PENGUIN BOOKS
A SEASON OF GHOSTS

Born in Kasauli, Himachal Pradesh, in 1934, Ruskin Bond grew up in Jamnagar (Gujarat), Dehradun and Simla. His first novel, *Room on the Roof*, written when he was seventeen, received the John Llewellyn Rhys Memorial Prize in 1957. Since then he has written over a hundred short stories, essays and novellas (including *Vagrants in the Valley* and *A Flight of Pigeons*) and more than thirty books for children. He has also published two volumes of autobiography, *Scenes from a Writer's Life*, which describes his formative years growing up in Anglo-India, and *The Lamp Is Lit*, a collection of essays and episodes from his journal. In 1992 he received the Sahitya Akademi award for English writing in India. He was awarded the Padma Shree in 1999.

Ruskin Bond lives with his adopted family in Mussoorie.

ALSO BY RUSKIN BOND

Penguin

The Room on the Roof, Vagrants in the Valley
Our Trees Still Grow in Dehra
The Night Train at Deoli
Time Stops at Shamli
Rain in the Mountains
Strangers in the Night
Scenes from a Writer's Life
The Lamp Is Lit
Delhi Is Not Far: The Best of Ruskin Bond
The Penguin Book of Indian Ghost Stories (ed.)
The Penguin Book of Indian Railway Stories (ed.)
The Penguin Book of Indian Love Stories and Lyrics (ed.)
Collected Fiction

Puffin

Panther's Moon and Other Stories
Room on the Roof

RUSKIN BOND

A Season of Ghosts

PENGUIN BOOKS

Penguin Books India (P) Ltd., 11 Community Centre, Panchsheel Park, New Delhi 110 017, India
Penguin Books Ltd., 27 Wrights Lane, London W8 5TZ, UK
Penguin Putnam Inc., 375 Hudson Street, New York, NY 10014, USA
Penguin Books Australia Ltd., Ringwood, Victoria, Australia
Penguin Books Canada Ltd., 10 Alcorn Avenue, Suite 300, Toronto, Ontario M4V 3B2, Canada
Penguin Books (NZ) Ltd., Cnr Rosedale and Airborne Roads, Albany, Auckland, New Zealand

First published in Viking by Penguin Books India 1999
First published in Penguin Books 2000

10 9 8 7 6 5 4 3 2 1

Typeset in *Sabon Roman* by SÜRYA, New Delhi
Printed at Chaman Offset Printers, New Delhi

Contents

Contents

Introduction

'SIR, DO YOU believe in ghosts?' asked a young student from a New Delhi school.

After giving this question some thought, I answered in all honesty, 'Well, I don't *believe* in them. But I keep *seeing* them!'

Seeing, they say, is believing, but I'm not so sure. You can see a magician or conjurer cut a man in half, but you will believe what you see only if he fails to put the two halves together again.

Anyway, here are some of the ghosts, phantoms, witches, demons and creatures of the night that I have seen, felt or conjured up.

Most of these stories were written during the last six months, which could rightly be called my 'dark' or 'supernatural' period. But over the years I have written the occasional ghost story, and I have been fascinated by the genre ever since I discovered the stories of M.R. James in a lonely forest bungalow when I was just ten or eleven. I went on to enjoy the supernatural tales of Algernon Blackwood, Hugh Walpole, H.G. Wells, Walter de la Mare, Sheridan Le Fanu, Kipling, and, in more recent times, Satyajit Ray. And a friend's mother, 'Bibiji', regaled me with tales of beautiful jinns and churels, mischievous bhuts and prets, and terrifying rakshasas.

I know some very sensible and practical people who have experienced the presence of ghosts. Mr Vishal Ohri, the manager of the State Bank in Mussoorie, tells me of a chandelier that rocks all night in one of the guest rooms. Mrs Goel, in Almora, feels a malignant presence whenever she climbs a certain flight of stairs. The ghost of Colonel Young, the founder of Landour, often turns up in Ganesh Saili's cottage—situated on Young's old Mullingar estate—and vanishes along with Mr Saili's pipe tobacco. H.H. Maharani Sahiba of Jind has a pet Pekinese, Guru Mai, who has been known to levitate. She ascends slowly toward the ceiling and then comes down again quite rapidly but without any injury to herself. Apparently she is possessed by a pisach, or evil spirit, although I have always found her to be a most affectionate little creature.

I don't think ghosts appear at random. They seem to favour places closely connected with their former existence in this world. Old houses, which have seen many people come and go, are often favourite haunts for the spirits of the departed. When I lived at Maplewood Lodge, there was a ghost who used to flitter through my bedroom late at night. I don't see it here at Ivy Cottage. Perhaps the noise of passing traffic frightens it away.

My old school, Bishop Cotton's in Shimla, had a ghost who walked the corridors at night—probably the same gentleman who had set the building on fire in the 1870s. My mother, who studied at the La Martiniere in Lucknow, told me of a haunted boxroom into which no one ever went alone. Most old schools have their ghosts. It's almost a tradition. As also with regimental parade grounds, which always have ghostly colonels on phantom horses; railway retiring rooms, where someone always waits for a train that never comes; and old dak bungalows, where you may be waited upon by a spectral khansama from the Raj days.

*

The novella included in this book is not a ghost story but rather a light-hearted attempt at writing a detective story. 'Who killed the Rani?' is set in the Mussoorie of twenty-odd years ago, when vehicles were a rarity in the hill station and even a police officer had to trudge around on aching feet. Although Mussoorie is not as placid and restful as it used to be, we have never really had a crime wave. Occasionally the corpse of a tourist tumbles out of a cupboard or turns up in a hotel boxbed, left behind by his erstwhile companions. The character and type of crime has changed over the years. Crimes of passion—as in my story—are rather old-fashioned. Today it's usually about money or property.

Inspector Keemat Lal, based on a police officer who had once befriended me, is no Holmes or Poirot; he is a bit of a plodder, but he gets there in the end. And he has what other brainy 'tecs seldom have—a vulnerable nature, a touch of humanity, a streak of compassion, which make him a nice man to know. One never feels overawed or uncomfortable in his presence.

And what of the 'Rani'? She existed too—a rather unfriendly neighbour, who was both feared and detested by those who had to deal with her. A witch of sorts, in fact. I put her in this story, making her the victim, while she was still alive, although I took the trouble to disguise her true identity. A year later she died, in mysterious circumstances. I felt bad about it at the time, though I hadn't really *wished* her dead. Was it just coincidence? Or presentiment? Or do our thoughts, if strong enough, sometimes influence external events? I hope not. But you never know . . .

Landour, Mussoorie   Ruskin Bond
November 1999

Whistling in the Dark

ॐ

THE MOON WAS almost at the full. Bright moonlight flooded the road. But I was stalked by the shadows of the trees, by the crooked oak branches reaching out towards me—some threateningly, others as though they needed companionship.

Once I dreamt that the trees could walk. That on moonlit nights like this they would uproot themselves for a while, visit each other, talk about old times—for they had seen many men and happenings, especially the older ones. And then, before dawn, they would return to the places where they had been condemned to grow. Lonely sentinels of the night. And this was a good night for them to walk. They appeared eager to do so: a restless rustling of leaves, the creaking of branches—these were sounds that came from within them in the silence of the night . . .

Occasionally other strollers passed me in the dark. It was still quite early, just eight o'clock, and some people were on their way home. Others were walking into town for a taste of the bright lights, shops and restaurants. On the unlit road I could not recognize them. They did not notice me. I was reminded of an old song from my childhood. Softly, I began humming the tune, and soon the words came back to me:

> We three,
> We're not a crowd;
> We're not even company—
> My echo,
> My shadow,
> And me . . .

I looked down at my shadow, moving silently beside me. We take our shadows for granted, don't we? There they are, the uncomplaining companions of a lifetime, mute and helpless witnesses to our every act of commission or omission. On this bright moonlit night I could not help noticing you, Shadow, and I was sorry that you had to see so much that I was ashamed of; but glad, too, that you were around when I had my small triumphs. And what of my echo? I thought of calling out to see if my call came back to me; but I refrained from doing so, as I did not wish to disturb the perfect stillness of the mountains or the conversations of the trees.

The road wound up the hill and levelled out at the top, where it became a ribbon of moonlight entwined between tall deodars. A flying squirrel glided across the road, leaving one tree for another. A nightjar called. The rest was silence.

The old cemetery loomed up before me. There were many old graves—some large and monumental—and there were a few recent graves too, for the cemetery was still in use. I could see flowers scattered on one of them—a few late dahlias and scarlet salvia. Further on, near the boundary wall, part of the cemetery's retaining wall had collapsed in the heavy monsoon rains. Some of the tombstones had come down with the wall. One grave lay exposed. A rotting coffin and a few scattered bones were the only relics of someone who had lived and loved like you and me.

Part of the tombstone lay beside the road, but the lettering had worn away. I am not normally a morbid person, but something made me stoop and pick up a smooth round shard of bone, probably part of a skull. When my hand closed over it, the bone crumbled into fragments. I let them fall to the grass. Dust to dust.

And from somewhere, not too far away, came the sound of someone whistling.

At first I thought it was another late-evening stroller, whistling to himself much as I had been humming my old song. But the whistler approached quite rapidly; the whistling was loud and cheerful. A boy on a bicycle sped past. I had only a glimpse of him, before his cycle went weaving through the shadows on the road.

But he was back again in a few minutes. And this time he stopped a few feet away from me, and gave me a quizzical half-smile. A slim dusky boy of fourteen or fifteen. He wore a school blazer and a yellow scarf. His eyes were pools of liquid moonlight.

'You don't have a bell on your cycle,' I said.

He said nothing, just smiled at me with his head a little to one side. I put out my hand, and I thought he was going to take it. But then, quite suddenly, he was off again, whistling cheerfully though rather tunelessly. A whistling schoolboy. A bit late for him to be out, but he seemed an independent sort.

The whistling grew fainter, then faded away altogether. A deep sound-denying silence fell upon the forest. My shadow and I walked home.

Next morning I woke to a different kind of whistling—the song of the thrush outside my window.

It was a wonderful day, the sunshine warm and

sensuous, and I longed to be out in the open. But there was work to be done, proofs to be corrected, letters to be written. And it was several days before I could walk to the top of the hill, to that lonely tranquil resting place under the deodars. It seemed to me ironic that those who had the best view of the glistening snow-capped peaks were all buried several feet underground.

Some repair work was going on. The retaining wall of the cemetery was being shored up, but the overseer told me that there was no money to restore the damaged grave. With the help of the chowkidar, I returned the scattered bones to a little hollow under the collapsed masonry, and I left some money with him so that he could have the open grave bricked up. The name on the gravestone had worn away, but I could make out a date—20 November 1950—some fifty years ago, but not too long ago as gravestones go . . .

I found the burial register in the church vestry and turned back the yellowing pages to 1950, when I was just a schoolboy myself. I found the name there—Michael Dutta, aged fifteen—and the cause of death: road accident.

Well, I could only make guesses. And to turn conjecture into certainty, I would have to find an old resident who might remember the boy or the accident.

There was old Miss Marley at Pine Top. A retired teacher from Woodstock, she had a wonderful memory, and she had lived in the hill station for more than half a century.

White-haired and smooth-cheeked, her bright blue eyes full of curiosity, she gazed benignly at me through her old-fashioned pince-nez.

'Michael was a charming boy—full of exuberance, always ready to oblige. I had only to mention that I needed a newspaper or an Aspirin, and he'd be off on his bicycle, swooping down these steep roads with great abandon. But these hills roads, with their sudden corners, weren't meant for racing around on a bicycle. They were widening our road for motor traffic, and a truck was coming uphill, loaded with rubble, when Michael came round a bend and smashed headlong into it. He was rushed to the hospital, and the doctors did their best, but he did not recover consciousness. Of course you must have seen his grave. That's why you're here. His parents? They left shortly afterwards. Went abroad, I think . . . A charming boy, Michael, but just a bit too reckless. You'd have liked him, I think.'

I did not see the phantom bicycle-rider again for some time, although I felt his presence on more than one occasion. And when, on a cold winter's evening, I walked past that lonely cemetery, I thought I heard him whistling far away. But he did not manifest himself. Perhaps it was only the echo of a whistle, in communion with my insubstantial shadow.

It was several months before I saw that smiling face again. And then it came at me out of the mist as I was walking home in drenching monsoon rain. I had been to a dinner party at the old community centre, and I was returning home along a very narrow, precipitous path known as the Eyebrow. A storm had been threatening all evening. A heavy mist had settled on the hillside. It was so thick that the light from my torch simply bounced off it. The sky blossomed with sheet lightning and thunder rolled over the mountains. The rain became heavier. I moved forward slowly, carefully, hugging the hillside. There was a clap of thunder, and then I saw him emerge from the mist and stand in my way—the same slim dark youth who had materialized near the cemetery. He did no. smile. Instead he put up his hand and waved me back. I hesitated, stood still. The mist lifted a little, and I saw that the path had disappeared. There was a gaping emptiness a few feet in front of me. And then a drop of over a hundred feet to the rocks below.

As I stepped back, clinging to a thorn bush for

support, the boy vanished. I stumbled back to the community centre and spent the night on a chair in the library.

I did not see him again.

But weeks later, when I was down with a severe bout of flu, I heard him from my sickbed, whistling beneath my window. Was he calling to me to join him, I wondered, or was he just trying to reassure me that all was well? I got out of bed and looked out, but I saw no one. From time to time I heard his whistling; but as I got better, it grew fainter until it ceased altogether.

Fully recovered, I renewed my old walks to the top of the hill. But although I lingered near the cemetery until it grew dark, and paced up and down the deserted road, I did not see or hear the whistler again. I felt lonely, in need of a friend, even if it was only a phantom bicycle-rider. But there were only the trees.

And so every evening I walk home in the darkness, singing the old refrain:

We three,
We're not alone,
We're not even company—
My echo,
My shadow,
And me . . .

10

Wilson's Bridge

කිරෝ

THE OLD WOODEN bridge has gone, and today an iron suspension bridge straddles the Bhagirathi as it rushes down the gorge below Gangotri. But villagers will tell you that you can still hear the hoofs of Wilson's horse as he gallops across the bridge he had built a hundred and fifty years ago. At the time people were sceptical of its safety, and so, to prove its sturdiness, he rode across it again and again. Parts of the old bridge can still be seen on the far bank of the river. And the legend of Wilson and his pretty hill bride, Gulabi, is still well-known in this region.

I had joined some friends in the old forest rest house near the river. There were the Rays, recently married, and the Dattas, married many years. The younger Rays quarrelled frequently; the older Dattas looked on with more amusement than concern. I was a part of their group and yet something of an outsider. As a single man, I was a person of no importance. And as a marriage counsellor, I wouldn't have been of any use to them.

I spent most of my time wandering along the river banks or exploring the thick deodar and oak forests that covered the slopes. It was these trees that had made a fortune for Wilson and his patron, the Raja of Tehri. They had exploited the great forests to the full, floating huge logs downstream to the timber yards in the plains.

Returning to the rest house late one evening, I was halfway across the bridge when I saw a figure at the other end, emerging from the mist. Presently I made out a woman, wearing the plain dhoti of the hills; her hair fell loose over her shoulders. She appeared not to see me, and reclined against the railing of the bridge, looking down at the rushing waters far below. And then, to my amazement and horror, she climbed over the railing and threw herself into the river.

I ran forward, calling out, but I reached the railing only to see her fall into the foaming waters below, where she was carried swiftly downstream.

The watchman's cabin stood a little way off. The door was open. The watchman, Ram Singh,

14

was reclining on his bed, smoking a hookah.

'Someone just jumped off the bridge,' I said breathlessly. 'She's been swept down the river!'

The watchman was unperturbed. 'Gulabi again,' he said, almost to himself; and then to me, 'Did you see her clearly?'

'Yes, a woman with long loose hair—but I didn't see her face very clearly.'

'It must have been Gulabi. Only a ghost, my dear sir. Nothing to be alarmed about. Every now and then someone sees her throw herself into the river. Sit down,' he said, gesturing towards a battered old armchair, 'be comfortable and I'll tell you all about it.'

I was far from comfortable, but I listened to Ram Singh tell me the tale of Gulabi's suicide. After making me a glass of hot sweet tea, he launched into a long rambling account of how Wilson, a British adventurer seeking his fortune, had been hunting musk deer when he encountered Gulabi on the path from her village. The girl's grey-green eyes and peach-blossom complexion enchanted him, and he went out of his way to get to know her people. Was he in love with her, or did he simply find her beautiful and desirable? We shall never really know. In the course of his travels and adventures he had known many women, but Gulabi was different, childlike and ingenuous, and he decided he would marry her. The humble family to which she belonged had no objection. Hunting had its limitations, and Wilson found it more profitable to trap the region's great forest wealth. In a few years he had made a fortune. He built a large timbered house at Harsil, another in Dehradun, and a third at Mussoorie. Gulabi had all she could have wanted, including two robust little sons. When he was away on work, she looked after their children and their large apple orchard at Harsil.

And then came the evil day when Wilson met the Englishwoman, Ruth, on the Mussoorie mall, and decided that she should have a share of his affections and his wealth. A fine house was provided for her too. The time he spent at Harsil with Gulabi and his children dwindled. 'Business affairs'—he was now one of the owners of a bank—kept him in the fashionable hill resort. He was a popular host and took his friends and associates on shikar parties in the Doon.

Gulabi brought up her children in village style. She heard stories of Wilson's dalliance with the Mussoorie woman and, on one of his rare visits, she confronted him and voiced her resentment, demanding that he leave the other woman. He brushed her aside and told her not to listen to idle gossip. When he turned away from her, she picked up the flintlock pistol that lay on the gun table, and fired one shot at him. The bullet missed him and shattered her looking glass. Gulabi ran out of the house, through the orchard and into the forest, then down the steep path to the bridge built by Wilson only two or three years before. When he had recovered his composure, he mounted his horse and came looking for her. It was too late. She had already thrown herself off the bridge into the swirling waters far below. Her body was found a mile or two downstream, caught between some rocks.

This was the tale that Ram Singh told me, with various flourishes and interpolations of his own. I thought it would make a good story to tell my friends that evening, before the fireside in the rest house. They found the story fascinating, but when I told them I had seen Gulabi's ghost, they thought I was doing a little embroidering of my own. Mrs Dutta thought it was a tragic tale. Young Mrs Ray thought Gulabi had been very silly. 'She was a simple girl,' opined Mr Dutta. 'She responded in the only way she knew . . .' 'Money can't buy happiness,' said Mr Ray. 'No,' said Mrs Dutta, 'but it can buy you a great many comforts.' Mrs Ray wanted to talk of other things, so I changed the subject. It can get a little confusing for a bachelor who must spend the evening with two married couples. There are undercurrents which he is aware of but not equipped to deal with.

I would walk across the bridge quite often after that. It was busy with traffic during the day, but after dusk there were only a few vehicles on the road and seldom any pedestrians. A mist rose from the gorge below and obscured the far end of the bridge. I preferred walking there in the evening, half-expecting, half-hoping to see Gulabi's ghost again. It was her face that I really wanted to see. Would she still be as beautiful as she was fabled to be?

It was on the evening before our departure that something happened that would haunt me for a long time afterwards.

There was a feeling of restiveness as our days there drew to a close. The Rays had apparently made up their differences, although they weren't talking very much. Mr Dutta was anxious to get back to his office in Delhi and Mrs Dutta's rheumatism was playing up. I was restless too, wanting to return to my writing desk in Mussoorie.

That evening I decided to take one last stroll across the bridge to enjoy the cool breeze of a summer's night in the mountains. The moon hadn't come up, and it was really quite dark, although there were lamps at either end of the bridge providing sufficient light for those who wished to cross over.

I was standing in the middle of the bridge, in the darkest part, listening to the river thundering down the gorge, when I saw the sari-draped figure emerging from the lamplight and making towards the railings.

Instinctively I called out, 'Gulabi!'

She half-turned towards me, but I could not see her clearly. The wind had blown her hair across her face and all I saw was wildly staring eyes. She raised herself over the railing and threw herself off the bridge. I heard the splash as her body struck the water far below.

Once again I found myself running towards the part of the railing where she had jumped. And then someone was running towards the same spot, from the direction of the rest house. It was young Mr Ray.

'My wife!' he cried out. 'Did you see my wife?'

He rushed to the railing and stared down at the swirling waters of the river.

'Look! There she is!' He pointed at a helpless figure bobbing about in the water.

We ran down the steep bank to the river but the current had swept her on. Scrambling over rocks and bushes, we made frantic efforts to catch up with the drowning woman. But the river in that defile is a roaring torrent, and it was over an hour before we were able to retrieve poor Mrs Ray's body, caught in driftwood about a mile downstream.

She was cremated not far from where we found her and we returned to our various homes in gloom and grief, chastened but none the wiser for the experience.

If you happen to be in that area and decide to cross the bridge late in the evening, you might see Gulabi's ghost or hear the hoofbeats of Wilson's horse as he canters across the old wooden bridge looking for her. Or you might see the ghost of Mrs Ray and hear her husband's anguished cry. Or there might be others. Who knows?

On Fairy Hill

಄಄಄

THOSE LITTLE GREEN lights that I used to see twinkling away on Pari Tibba—there had to be a scientific explanation for them. I was sure of that. After dark we see or hear many things that seem mysterious and irrational. And then, by the clear light of day, we find that the magic and the mystery have an explanation after all.

I saw those lights occasionally, late at night, when I walked home from the town to my little cottage at the edge of the forest. They moved too fast to be torches or lanterns carried by people. And as there were no roads on Pari Tibba, they could not have been cycle or cart lamps. Someone told me there was phosphorus in the rocks and that this probably accounted for the luminous glow emanating from the hillside late at night. Possibly, but I was not convinced.

My encounter with the little people happened by the light of day.

One morning early in April, purely on an impulse, I decided to climb to the top of Pari Tibba and look around for myself. It was springtime in the Himalayan foothills. The sap was rising—in the trees, in the grass, in the wildflowers, in my own veins. I took the path through the oak forest, down to the little stream at the foot of the hill, and then up the steep slope of Pari Tibba, Hill of Fairies.

It was quite a scramble to get to the top. The path ended at the stream at the bottom of the slope. I had to clutch at brambles and tufts of grass to make the ascent. Fallen pine needles, slippery underfoot, made it difficult to get a foothold. But finally I made it to the top—a grassy plateau fringed by pines and a few wild medlar trees now clothed in white blossom.

It was a pretty spot. And as I was hot and sweaty, I removed most of my clothing and lay down under a medlar to rest. The climb had been quite tiring. But a fresh breeze soon revived me. It made a soft humming sound in the pines. And the grass, sprinkled with yellow buttercups, buzzed with the sound of crickets and grasshoppers.

After some time, I stood up and surveyed the

scene. To the north, Landour with its rusty red-roofed cottages; to the south, the wide valley and a silver stream flowing towards the Ganga. To the west were rolling hills, patches of forest and a small village tucked into a fold of the mountain.

Disturbed by my presence, a barking deer ran across the clearing and down the opposite slope. A band of long-tailed blue magpies rose from the oak trees, glided across the knoll, and settled in another copse of oaks.

I was alone, alone with the wind and the sky. It had probably been months, possibly years, since any human had passed that way. The soft lush grass looked most inviting. I lay down again on the sun-warmed sward. Pressed and bruised by my weight, the catmint and clover in the grass gave out a soft fragrance. A ladybird climbed up my leg and began to explore my body. A swarm of white butterflies fluttered around me.

I slept.

I have no idea how long I slept. When I awoke, it was to experience an unusual soothing sensation all over my limbs, as though they were being gently stroked with rose petals.

All lethargy gone, I opened my eyes to find a little girl—or was it a woman?—about two inches tall, sitting cross-legged on my chest and studying me intently. Her hair fell in long black tresses. Her skin was the colour of honey. Her firm little breasts were like tiny acorns. She held a buttercup, which was larger than her hand, and she was stroking my skin with it.

I was tingling all over. A sensation of sensual joy surged through my limbs.

A tiny boy—man?—also naked, now joined the elfin girl, and they held hands and looked into my eyes, smiling. Their teeth were like little pearls, their lips soft petals of apricot blossom. Were these the nature spirits, the flower fairies, I had often dreamt of?

I raised my head, and saw that there were scores of little people all over me. The delicate and gentle creatures were exploring my legs, arms and body with caressing gestures. Some of them were laving me with dew or pollen or some other soft essence. I closed my eyes again. Waves of pure physical pleasure swept over me. I had never known anything like it. It was endless, all-embracing. My limbs turned to water. The sky revolved around me, and I must have fainted.

When I came to, perhaps an hour later, the little people had gone. The fragrance of honeysuckle lingered in the air. A deep rumble overhead made me look up. Dark clouds had gathered, threatening rain. Had the thunder frightened them away to their abode beneath the rocks and roots? Or had they simply tired of sporting with an unknown newcomer? Mischievous they were; for when I looked around for my clothes I could not find them anywhere.

A wave of panic surged over me. I ran here and there, looking behind shrubs and tree trunks, but to no avail. My clothes had disappeared, along with the fairies—if indeed they were fairies!

It began to rain. Large drops cannoned off the dry rocks. Then it hailed, and soon the slope was covered with ice. There was no shelter. Naked, I clambered down as far as the stream. There was no one to see me—except for a wild mountain goat speeding away in the opposite direction. Gusts of wind slashed rain and hail across my face and body. Panting and shivering, I took shelter beneath an overhanging rock until the storm had passed. By then it was almost dusk, and I was able to ascend the path to my cottage without encountering anyone, apart from a band of startled langoors who chattered excitedly on seeing me.

I couldn't stop shivering, so I went straight to bed. I slept a deep dreamless sleep through the afternoon, evening and night, and woke up next morning with a high fever.

Mechanically I dressed, made myself some breakfast and tried to get through the morning's chores. When I took my temperature, I found it was 104. So I swallowed a Brufen and went back to bed.

There I lay till late afternoon, when the postman's knocking woke me. I left my letters unopened on my desk—breaking a sacrosanct ritual—and returned to my bed.

The fever lasted almost a week and left me weak and feeble. I couldn't have climbed Pari Tibba again even if I'd wanted to. But I reclined on my window seat and looked at the clouds drifting over that bleak hill. Desolate it seemed, and yet strangely inhabited. When it grew dark, I waited for those little green fairy lights to appear; but these, it seemed, were now to be denied to me.

And so I returned to my desk, my typewriter, my newspaper articles and correspondence. It was a lonely period in my life. My marriage hadn't worked out: my wife, fond of high society and averse to living with an unsuccessful writer in a remote cottage in the woods, was pursuing her own, more successful career in Mumbai. I had always been rather half-hearted in my approach to making money, whereas she had always wanted more and more of it. She left me—left me with my books and my dreams . . .

Had it all been a dream, that strange episode on Pari Tibba? Had a too-active imagination conjured up those aerial spirits, those siddhas of the upper air? Or were they underground people, living deep within the bowels of the hill? If I was going to preserve my sanity, I knew I had better get on with the more mundane aspects of living—going into town to buy groceries, mending the leaking roof, paying the electricity bill, plodding up to the post office, and remembering to deposit the odd cheque that came my way. All the routine things that made life so dull and dreary.

The truth is, what we commonly call life is not really living at all. The regular and settled ways which we accept as the course of life are really the curse of life. They tie us down to the trivial and monotonous, and we will do almost anything to get away, ideally for a more exalted and fulfilling existence, but if that is not possible, for a few hours of forgetfulness in alcohol, drugs, forbidden sex or even golf. So it would give me great joy to go underground with the fairies. Those little people who have sought refuge in Mother Earth from mankind's killing ways are as vulnerable as butterflies and flowers. All things beautiful are easily destroyed.

I am sitting at my window in the gathering dark, penning these stray thoughts, when I see them coming—hand-in-hand, walking on a swirl of mist, suffused with all the radiant colours of the rainbow. For a rainbow has formed a bridge for them from Pari Tibba to the edge of my window.

I am ready to go with them to their secret lairs or to the upper air—far from the stifling confines of the world in which we toil . . .

Come, fairies, carry me away, to experience again the perfection I did that summer's day!

The Black Cat

ଔଓଔ

BEFORE THE CAT came, of course there had to be a broomstick.

In the bazaar of one of our hill stations is an old junk shop—dirty, dingy and dark—in which I often potter about looking for old books or Victorian bric-a-brac. Sometimes one comes across useful household items, but I do not usually notice these. I was, however, attracted to an old but well-preserved broom standing in a corner of the shop. A long-handled broom was just what I needed. I had no servant to sweep out the rooms of my cottage, and I did not enjoy bending over double when using the common short-handled jharoo.

The old broom was priced at ten rupees. I haggled with the shopkeeper and got it for five.

It was a strong broom, full of character, and I

used it to good effect almost every morning. And there this story might have ended—or would never have begun—if I had not found the large black cat sitting on the garden wall.

The black cat had bright yellow eyes, and it gave me a long penetrating look, as though it were summing up my possibilities as an exploitable human. Though it miaowed once or twice, I paid no attention. I did not care much for cats. But when I went indoors, I found that the cat had followed and begun scratching at the pantry door.

It must be hungry, I thought, and gave it some milk.

The cat lapped up the milk, purring deeply all the while, then sprang up on a cupboard and made itself comfortable.

Well, for several days there was no getting rid of that cat. It seemed completely at home, and merely tolerated my presence in the house. It was more interested in my broom than me, and would dance and skittle around the broom whenever I was sweeping the rooms. And when the broom was resting against the wall, the cat would sidle up to it, rubbing itself against the handle and purring loudly.

A cat and a broomstick—the combination was suggestive, full of possibilities . . . The cottage was old, almost a hundred years old, and I wondered about the kind of tenants it might have had during these long years. I had been in the cottage only for a year. And though it stood alone in the midst of a forest of Himalayan oaks, I had never encountered any ghosts or spirits.

Miss Bellows came to see me in the middle of July. I heard the tapping of a walking stick on the rocky path outside the cottage, a tapping which stopped near the gate.

'Mr Bond!' called an imperious voice. 'Are you at home?'

I had been doing some gardening, and looked up to find an elderly straight-backed Englishwoman peering at me over the gate.

'Good evening,' I said, dropping my hoe.

'I believe you have my cat,' said Miss Bellows.

Though I had not met the lady before, I knew her by name and reputation. She was the oldest resident in the hill station.

'I do have a cat,' I said, 'though it's probably more correct to say that the cat has me. If it's your cat, you're welcome to it. Why don't you come in while I look for her?'

Miss Bellows stepped in. She wore a rather old-fashioned black dress, and her ancient but strong walnut stick had two or three curves in it and a knob instead of a handle.

35

She made herself comfortable in an armchair while I went in search of the cat. But the cat was on one of her mysterious absences, and though I called for her in my most persuasive manner, she did not respond. I knew she was probably quite near. But cats are like that—perverse obstinate creatures.

When finally I returned to the sitting room, there was the cat, curled up on Miss Bellows' lap.

'Well, you've got her, I see. Would you like some tea before you go?'

'No, thank you,' said Miss Bellows. 'I don't drink tea.'

'Something stronger, perhaps. A little brandy?' She looked up at me rather sharply. Disconcerted, I hastened to add, 'Not that I drink much, you know. I keep a little in the house for emergencies. It helps ward off colds and things. It's particularly good for—er—well, for colds,' I finished lamely.

'I see your kettle's boiling,' she said. 'Can I have some hot water?'

'Hot water? Certainly.' I was a little puzzled, but I did not want to antagonize Miss Bellows at our first meeting.

'Thank you. And a glass.'

She took the glass and I went to get the kettle. From the pocket of her voluminous dress, she extracted two small packets, similar to those

36

containing chemists' powders. Opening both packets, she poured first a purple powder and then a crimson powder into the glass. Nothing happened.

'Now the water, please,' she said.

'It's boiling hot!'

'Never mind.'

I poured boiling water into her glass, and there was a terrific fizzing and bubbling as the frothy stuff rose to the rim. It gave off a horrible stench. The potion was so hot that I thought it would crack the glass; but before this could happen, Miss Bellows put it to her lips and drained the contents.

'I think I'll be going now,' she said, putting the glass down and smacking her lips. The cat, tail in the air, voiced its agreement. Said Miss Bellows, 'I'm much obliged to you, young man.'

'Don't mention it,' I said humbly. 'Always at your service.'

She gave me her thin bony hand, and held mine in an icy grip.

I saw Miss Bellows and the black cat to the gate, and returned pensively to my sitting room. Living alone was beginning to tell on my nerves and imagination. I made a half-hearted attempt to laugh at my fancies, but the laugh stuck in my throat. I couldn't help noticing that the broom was missing from its corner.

I dashed out of the cottage and looked up and down the path. There was no one to be seen. In the gathering darkness I could hear Miss Bellows' laughter, followed by a snatch of song:

> With the darkness round me growing,
> And the moon behind my hat,
> You will soon have trouble knowing
> Which is witch and witch's cat.

Something whirred overhead like a Diwali rocket.

I looked up and saw them silhouetted against the rising moon. Miss Bellows and her cat were riding away on my broomstick.

Reunion at the Regal

చ౦ఙ

IF YOU WANT to see a ghost, just stand outside New Delhi's Regal Cinema for twenty minutes or so. The approach to the grand old cinema hall is a great place for them. Sooner or later you'll see a familiar face in the crowd. Before you have time to recall who it was or who it may be, it will have disappeared and you will be left wondering if it really was so-and-so . . . because surely so-and-so died several years ago . . .

The Regal was very posh in the early 1940s when, in the company of my father, I saw my first film there. The Connaught Place cinemas still had a new look about them, and they showed the latest offerings from Hollywood and Britain. To see a Hindi film, you had to travel all the way to Kashmere Gate or Chandni Chowk.

Over the years, I was in and out of the Regal quite a few times, and so I became used to meeting old acquaintances or glimpsing familiar faces in the foyer or on the steps outside.

On one occasion, I was mistaken for a ghost.

I was about thirty at the time. I was standing on the steps of the arcade, waiting for someone, when a young Indian man came up to me and said something in German or what sounded like German.

'I'm sorry,' I said. 'I don't understand. You may speak to me in English or Hindi.'

'Aren't you Hans? We met in Frankfurt last year.'

'I'm sorry, I've never been to Frankfurt.'

'You look exactly like Hans.'

'Maybe I'm his double. Or maybe I'm his ghost!'

My facetious remark did not amuse the young man. He looked confused and stepped back, a look of horror spreading over his face. 'No, no,' he stammered. 'Hans is alive, you can't be his ghost!'

'I was only joking.'

But he had turned away, hurrying off through the crowd. He seemed agitated. I shrugged philosophically. So I had a double called Hans, I reflected, perhaps I'd run into him some day.

I mention this incident only to show that most of us have lookalikes, and that sometimes we see what we *want* to see, or are looking for, even if on looking closer, the resemblance isn't all that striking.

But there was no mistaking Kishen when he approached me. I hadn't seen him for five or six years, but he looked much the same. Bushy eyebrows, offset by gentle eyes; a determined chin, offset by a charming smile. The girls had always liked him, and he knew it; and he was content to let them do the pursuing.

We saw a film—I think it was *The Wind Cannot Read*—and then we strolled across to the old Standard Restaurant, ordered dinner and talked about old times, while the small band played sentimental tunes from the 1950s.

Yes, we talked about old times—growing up in Dehra, where we lived next door to each other, exploring our neighbours' lychee orchards, cycling about the town in the days before the scooter had been invented, kicking a football around on the maidan, or just sitting on the compound wall doing nothing. I had just finished school, and an entire year stretched before me until it was time to go abroad. Kishen's father, a civil engineer, was under transfer orders, so Kishen too temporarily did not have to go to school.

He was an easy-going boy, quite content to be

at a loose end in my company—I was to describe a couple of our escapades in my first novel, *The Room on the Roof*. I had literary pretensions; he was apparently without ambition although, as he grew older, he was to surprise me by his wide reading and erudition.

One day, while we were cycling along the bank of the Raipur canal, he skidded off the path and fell into the canal with his cycle. The water was only waist-deep; but it was quite swift, and I had to jump in to help him. There was no real danger, but we had some difficulty getting the cycle out of the canal.

Later, he learnt to swim.

But that was after I'd gone away . . .

Convinced that my prospects would be better in England, my mother packed me off to her relatives in Jersey, and it was to be four long years before I could return to the land I truly cared for. In that time, many of my Dehra friends had left the town; it wasn't a place where you could do much after finishing school. Kishen wrote to me from Calcutta, where he was at an engineering college. Then he was off to 'study abroad'. I heard from him from time to time. He seemed happy. He had an equable temperament and got on quite well with most people. He had a girlfriend too, he told me.

'But,' he wrote, 'you're my oldest and best friend. Wherever I go, I'll always come back to see you.'

And of course he did. We met several times while I was living in Delhi, and once we revisited Dehra together and walked down Rajpur Road and ate tikkees and golguppas behind the clock tower. But the old familiar faces were missing. The streets were overbuilt and overcrowded, and the lychee gardens were fast disappearing. After we got back to Delhi, Kishen accepted the offer of a job in Mumbai. We kept in touch in desultory fashion, but our paths and our lives had taken different directions. He was busy nurturing his career with an engineering firm; I had retreated to the hills with radically different goals—to write and be free of the burden of a ten-to-five desk job.

Time went by, and I lost track of Kishen.

About a year ago, I was standing in the lobby of the India International Centre, when an attractive young woman in her mid-thirties came up to me and said, 'Hello, Rusty, don't you remember me? I'm Manju. I lived next to you and Kishen and Ranbir when we were children.'

I recognized her then, for she had always been a pretty girl, the 'belle' of Dehra's Astley Hall.

We sat down and talked about old times and new times, and I told her that I hadn't heard from Kishen for a few years.

'Didn't you know?' she asked. 'He died about two years ago.'

'What happened?' I was dismayed, even angry, that I hadn't heard about it. 'He couldn't have been more than thirty-eight.'

'It was an accident on a beach in Goa. A child had got into difficulties and Kishen swam out to save her. He did rescue the little girl, but when he swam ashore he had a heart attack. He died right there on the beach. It seems he had always had a weak heart. The exertion must have been too much for him.'

I was silent. I knew he'd become a fairly good swimmer, but I did not know about the heart.

'Was he married?' I asked.

'No, he was always the eligible bachelor boy.'

It had been good to see Manju again, even though she had given me bad news. She told me she was happily married, with a small son. We promised to keep in touch.

And that's the end of this tale, apart from my brief visit to Delhi last November.

I had taken a taxi to Connaught Place and decided to get down at the Regal. I stood there a while, undecided about what to do or where to go. It was almost time for a show to start, and there were a lot of people milling around.

I thought someone called my name. I looked around, and there was Kishen in the crowd.

'Kishen!' I called, and started after him.

But a stout lady climbing out of a scooter rickshaw got in my way, and by the time I had a clear view again, my old friend had disappeared.

Had I seen his lookalike, a double? Or had he kept his promise to come back to see me once more?

Something in the Water

෨෨

I DISCOVERED THE pool near Rajpur on a hot summer's day some fifteen years ago. It was shaded by close-growing sal trees, and looked cool and inviting. I took off my clothes and dived in.

The water was colder than I had expected. It was an icy glacial cold. The sun never touched it for long, I supposed. Striking out vigorously, I swam to the other end of the pool and pulled myself up on the rocks, shivering.

But I wanted to swim some more. So I dived in again and did a gentle breaststroke towards the middle of the pool. Something slid between my legs. Something slimy, pulpy. I could see no one, hear nothing. I swam away, but the slippery floating thing followed me. I did not like it. Something curled around my leg. Not an underwater plant. Something that sucked at my foot. A long tongue

licked my calf. I struck out wildly, thrust myself
away from whatever it was that sought my company.
Something lonely, lurking in the shadows. Kicking
up spray, I swam like a frightened porpoise fleeing
from some terror of the deep.

Safely out of the water, I found a warm sunny
rock and stood there looking down at the water.

Nothing stirred. The surface of the pool was
now calm and undisturbed. Just a few fallen leaves
floating around. Not a frog, not a fish, not a
waterbird in sight. And that in itself seemed strange.
For you would have expected some sort of pond
life to have been in evidence.

But something lived in the pool, of that I was
sure. Something very cold-blooded, colder and wetter
than the water. Could it have been a corpse trapped
in the weeds? I did not want to know; so I dressed
and hurried away.

A few days later I left for Delhi, where I went
to work in an ad agency, telling people how to beat
the summer heat by drinking fizzy drinks that made
you more thirsty. The pool in the forest was
forgotten.

It was ten years before I visited Rajpur again.
Leaving the small hotel where I was staying, I
found myself walking through the same old sal
forest, drawn almost irresistibly towards the pool
where I had not been able to finish my swim. I was

not over-eager to swim there again, but I was curious to know if the pool still existed.

Well, it was there all right, although the surroundings had changed and a number of new houses and other buildings had come up where formerly there had only been wilderness. And there was a fair amount of activity in the vicinity of the pool.

A number of labourers were busy with buckets and rubber pipes, draining water from the pool. They had also dammed off and diverted the little stream that fed it.

Overseeing this operation was a well-dressed man in a white safari suit. I thought at first that he was an honorary forest warden, but it turned out that he was the owner of a new school that had been set up nearby.

'Do you live in Rajpur?' he asked.

'I used to . . . Once upon a time . . . Why are you emptying the pool?'

'It's become a hazard,' he said. 'Two of my boys were drowned here recently. Both senior students. Of course they weren't supposed to be swimming here without permission, the pool is off-limits. But you know what boys are like. Make a rule and they feel duty-bound to break it.'

He told me his name was Kapoor, and led me back to his house, a newly-built bungalow with a wide cool veranda. His servant brought us glasses of cold sherbet. We sat in cane chairs overlooking the pool and the forest. Across a clearing, a gravelled road led to the school buildings, newly whitewashed and glistening in the sun.

'Were the boys there at the same time?' I asked.

'Yes, they were friends. And they must have been attacked by absolute fiends. Limbs twisted and broken, faces disfigured. But death was due to drowning—that was the verdict of the medical examiner.'

We gazed down at the shallows of the pool, where a couple of men were still at work, the others having gone for their midday meal.

'Perhaps it would be better to leave the place alone,' I said. 'Put a barbed wire fence around it. Keep your boys away. Thousands of years ago, this valley was an inland sea. A few small pools and streams are all that is left of it.'

'I want to fill it in and build something there. An open-air theatre, maybe. We can always create an artificial pond somewhere else.'

Presently only one man remained at the pool, knee-deep in muddy churned-up water. And Mr Kapoor and I both saw what happened next.

Something rose out of the bottom of the pool. It looked like a giant snail, but its head was part-human, its body and limbs part-squid or octopus.

An enormous succubus. Its stood taller than the man in the pool. A creature soft and slimy, a survivor from our primaeval past.

With a great sucking motion, it enveloped the man completely so that only his arms and legs could be seen thrashing about wildly and futilely. The succubus dragged him down under the water.

Kapoor and I left the veranda and ran to the edge of the pool. Bubbles rose from the green scum near the surface. All was still and silent. And then, like bubblegum issuing from the mouth of a child, the mangled body of the man shot out of the water and came spinning towards us.

Dead and drowned and sucked dry of its fluids. place

Naturally no more work was done at the pool. The story was put out that the labourer had slipped and fallen to his death on the rocks. Kapoor swore me to secrecy. His school would have to close down if there were too many strange drownings and accidents in its vicinity. But he walled the place off from his property and made it practically inaccessible. The dense undergrowth of the sal forest now hides the approach.

The monsoon rains came and the pool filled up again.

I can tell you how to get there if you'd like to see it. But I wouldn't advise you to go for a swim.

The Prize

THEY WERE UP late, drinking in the old Ritz bar, and by one a.m. everyone was pretty well sloshed. Ganesh got into his electric blue Zen and zigzagged home. Victor drove off in his antique Morris Minor, which promptly broke down, forcing him to transfer to a taxi. Nandu, the proprietor, limped off to his cottage, a shooting pain in his foot presaging another attack of gout. Begum Tara, who had starred in over a hundred early talkies, climbed into a cycle rickshaw that had no driver, which hardly mattered as she promptly fell asleep. The bartender vanished into the night. Only Rahul, the romantic young novelist, remained in the foyer, wondering where everyone had gone and why he had been left behind.

The rooms were full. There wasn't a spare bed

in the hotel, for it was the height of the season and the hill station's hotels were overflowing. The room boys and kitchen staff had gone to their quarters. Only the night chowkidar's whistle could occasionally be heard as the retired havildar prowled around the estate.

The young writer felt he had been unfairly abandoned, and rather resented the slight. He'd been the life and soul of the party—or so he'd thought—telling everyone about the huge advance he'd just got for his latest book and how it was a certainty for the Booker Prize. He hadn't noticed their yawns; or if he had, he'd put it down to the lack of oxygen in the bar. It had been named the Horizontal Bar by one of the patrons, because of a tendency on the part of some of the clientele to fall asleep on the carpet—that very same carpet on which the Duke of Savoy had passed out exactly a hundred years ago.

Rahul had no intention of passing out on the floor. But his libations had made lying down somewhere seem quite imperative. A billiard table would have been fine, but the billiard room was locked. He staggered down the corridor; not a sofa or easy chair came into view. Finally, he found a door that opened, leading to the huge empty dining room, now lit only by a single electric bulb.

The old piano did not look too inviting, but the long dining table had been cleared of everything except a curry-stained tablecloth left there to do duty again at breakfast. Rahul managed to hoist himself up on the table and stretch himself out. It made a hard bed, and already stray breadcrumbs were irritating his tender skin, but he was too tired to care. The light bulb directly above him also failed to bother him too much. Although there was no air in the room, the bulb swayed slightly, as though an invisible hand had tapped it gently.

For an hour he slept, a deep dreamless sleep, and then he became vaguely aware of music, voices, footsteps and laughter. Someone was playing the piano. Chairs were pulled back. Glasses tinkled. Knives and forks clattered against dinner plates.

Rahul opened his eyes to find a banquet in progress. On *his* table—the table he was lying on, now flanked by huge tureens of food! And the diners were seemingly unaware of his presence. The men wore old-fashioned dress suits with bow ties and high collars; the women wore long flounced dresses with tight bodices that showed their ample bosoms to good advantage. Out of long habit, Rahul's hand automatically reached out for the nearest breast, and for once he did not receive a stinging slap; for the simple reason that his hands, if they were there at all, hadn't moved.

Someone said, 'Roast pig—I've been looking forward to this!' and stuck a knife and fork into Rahul's thigh.

He cried out, or tried to, but no one heard; he could not hear his own voice. He found he could raise his head and look down the length of his body, and he saw he had pig's trotters instead of his own feet.

Someone turned him over and sliced a bit off his rump.

'A most tender leg of pork,' remarked a woman on his left.

A fork jabbed him in the buttocks. Then a giant of a man, top-hatted, with a carving knife in his hand, leant over him. He wore a broad white apron, and on it was written in large letters CHAIRMAN OF THE JURY. The carving knife glistened in the lamplight.

Rahul screamed and leapt off the table. He fell against the piano, recovered his balance, dashed past the revellers, and out of the vast dining room.

He ran down the silent hotel corridor, banging on all the doors. But none opened to him. Finally, at Room No. 12A—hotels do not like using the number 13—the door gave way. Out of breath, shaking all over, our hero stumbled into the room and bolted the door behind him.

It was a single room with a single bed. The bedclothes appeared to be in some disarray but Rahul hardly noticed. All he wanted was to end the nightmare he had been having and get some sleep. Kicking off his shoes, he climbed into the bed fully dressed.

He had been lying there for at least five minutes before he realized that he wasn't alone in the bed. There was someone lying beside him, covered by a sheet. Rahul switched on the bedside lamp. Nothing moved, the body lay still. On the sheet, in large letters, were the words: BETTER LUCK NEXT TIME.

He pulled the sheet back and stared down at his own dead self.

Night of the Millennium

৭০৫৪

JACKALS HOWLED DISMALLY, foraging for bones and offal down in the khud below the butcher's shop. Pasand was unperturbed by the sound. A robust young computer whiz-kid and patriotic multinational, he prided himself on being above and beyond all superstitious fears of the unknown. In his lexicon, the unknown was just something that was waiting to be discovered. Hence this walk past the old cemetery late at night.

Midnight would see the new millennium in. The year 2000 beckoned, full of bright prospects for well-heeled young men like Pasand. True, there were millions—soon to be over a billion—sweating it out in the heat and dust of the plains below, scraping together a meagre living for themselves and their sprawling families. Not for them the advantages of a public school education, three cars in the garage, and a bank account in Bermuda. Ah well, mused Pasand, not everyone could have the brains and good luck, as well as inherited family wealth of course, that had made life so pleasant and promising for him. This was going to be the century in which the smart-asses would get to the top and all other varieties of asses would sink to the bottom. It was important to have a ruling elite, according to his philosophy; only then could slaves prosper!

He looked at his watch. It was just past midnight. He had eaten well, and he was enjoying his little walk along the lonely winding road which took him past the houses of the rich and famous, the Lals, the Banerjees, the Kapoors, the Ramchandanis—he was as good as any of them! Better, in fact. He was approaching his own personal Everest, while they had reached theirs and were on the downward slope, or so he presumed.

Here was the cemetery with its broken old tombstones, some of them dating from a hundred and fifty years ago: pathetic reminders of a once-powerful empire, now reduced to dust and crumbling monuments. Here lay colonels and magistrates, merchants and memsahibs, and many small children; fragile lives which had been snuffed out in more turbulent times. To Pasand, they were losers, all of them. He had nothing but contempt for those who hadn't been able to hang on to their power and glory. No lost empires for him!

The road here was very dark, for the trees grew thick on the northern slopes. Pasand felt a twinge of nervousness, but he was reassured by the feel of the cellphone in his pocket—he could always summon his driver or his armed bodyguard to come and pick him up.

The moon had risen over Nag Tibba, and the graves stood out in serried rows, as though forming a guard of honour for this modern knight in T-shirt and designer jeans. Through the deodars he saw a faint light on the perimeter of the cemetery. Here, he had learnt from one of his *chamchas*, lived a widow with a brood of small children. Although in poor health, she was still young and comely, and known to be lavish with her favours to those who were generous with their purses; for she needed the money for her hungry family.

She was also a little mad, they said, and preferred to sleep in one of the old domed tombs rather than in the quarters provided for her late husband, who had been the caretaker.

This did not bother Pasand. He was in search of sensual pleasure, not romance. And right now he felt an urgent need to exert his dominance over someone, preferably a woman, for he had to prove his manhood in some way. So far, most young women had shied away from his vainglorious and clumsy approach.

This woman wasn't young. She was in her late thirties, and poverty, malnutrition and ill-use had made her look much older. But there were vestiges of beauty in her smouldering eyes and sinewy limbs. Her gypsy blood must have had something to do with it. Her teeth gleamed in the darkness as she smiled at Pasand and invited him into her boudoir—the spacious tomb that she favoured most.

Pasand had no time for tender love-play. Clumsily he clawed at her breasts but found they were not much larger than his own. He tore at her already tattered clothes, pressed his mouth hungrily to her dry lips. She made no attempt to resist. He had his way. Then, while he lay supine across the cold damp slab of a grave that covered the remains of some long-dead warrior, she leaned over him and bit him on the cheek and neck.

He cried out in pain and astonishment, and tried to sit up. But a number of hands, small but strong, thrust him back against the tombstone. Small mouths, sharp teeth, pressed against his flesh. Muddy fingers tore at his clothes. Those young teeth bit—and bit again. His screams mingled with the cries of the jackals.

'Patience, my children, patience,' crooned the woman. 'There is more than enough for all of you.'

They feasted.

Down in the ravine, the jackals started howling again, awaiting their turn. The bones would be theirs. Only the cellphone would be rejected.

The Rakshasas

৯০৭

HERE, THEN, IS a tale of the mountain kingdoms. I heard it from Bibiji, my neighbour, as she sat smoking her hookah on the veranda. Bibi came from a village in the foothills, where ghosts and sprites and rakshasas—forty-yard-long demons able to change their shape at will—were still known to exist. She heard this story from her grandfather, whose reputation for veracity was impeccable.

In a village in the foothills there lived seven goldsmiths, well-known for their excellent workmanship. One day a powerful nobleman from a neighbouring kingdom sent them a message, asking them to come to his kingdom and make some ornaments for his wife. The seven goldsmiths, good friends, started out for the palace of this chief, which they reached after an arduous journey over seven hills. The chief was a sullen unsociable man, with a harelip that showed the pink gums above his teeth. The goldsmiths were uneasy in his presence; but as they had been promised a handsome reward for their work, they decided to do the job.

The chief conducted them into a large room where everything was ready for them to begin work. 'This is where you will work,' he said. After they examined the furnace, blowpipes and charcoal, he led them to another room. This room was bare, overlooking barren crags, with a long bedstead and a she-goat. The goldsmiths looked askance at one another, but the chief said, 'This is your sleeping room. You will retire into this room after work every night. Your supper will be the milk of this generous goat, and you will sleep on that bed which is large enough to accomodate all of you. Though you will have no food other than the milk, you will find it as nourishing as the most richly cooked dishes. Her milk strengthens the body and sharpens the intellect, and she will yield sufficient for all of you. But remember, you must finish your work within seven days.'

The goldsmiths did not relish the situation nor were they impressed by the arrangements that had been made. Nevertheless they set to work, and completed a good portion of it by the end of the first day. After changing their clothes, they milked the goat and began their supper. They found that their employer had not exaggerated the virtues of the goat, for her milk was very sweet and delicious. They had never tasted anything quite like it. As soon as they had drunk their fill, they were overcome by a strange exhileration. This was succeeded by drowsiness and they soon fell asleep. The bed was a little too small for all seven of them, but it was big enough to accomodate six. One of the goldsmiths agreed to sleep on the ground.

It was almost midnight when the goat began to lick the soles of the goldsmith who lay asleep on the floor. Slowly and with great relish, the goat sucked up the entire lifeblood of the unfortunate artisan, and the man died in his sleep.

Gradually a strange blue light filled the room, and the chief entered and said, 'Sister, are you happy? Sister, have you had enough?'

The goat replied, 'Brother rakshasa, you know I am happy as long as you can satisfy my hunger with human blood.' And then there was a clap of thunder, and both the chief and the goldsmith's corpse disappeared.

When the goldsmiths awoke the next morning and found one of their comrades missing, they were filled with grave misgivings. But they worked all the harder to complete that day's quota of work. And at night, after they dined again on the milk of the goat, they found the bed had contracted in breadth, and now only five persons could lie on it. The sixth had to stretch himself out on the ground. They fell once more into a deep sleep.

Once again, at midnight, the goat drank deeply of the blood of the sleeping goldsmith. The chief appeared, the same conversation took place between him and the goat, and then he and the corpse disappeared.

The remaining goldsmiths were quite alarmed when they awoke. But they were afraid to offend the chief and they were unwilling to lose the reward that had been promised them. And there were now fewer to share it. But when, after spending three more nights in the palace, only two of the seven goldsmiths were left, one of them told the other, 'Friend, let us sleep with our chotis, tied together'— for like all good goldsmiths they retained these tufts of hair in the middle of their shaven pates—'so that one may not vanish without awakening the other.'

That night the bed could only accommodate one person, so the second slept on the ground, but with his choti tied to that of his friend on the bed. At midnight, after the goat feasted on the blood of the sleeping man, the chief appeared promptly and asked, 'Sister, are you happy? Is your hunger appeased?'

'I am happy, brother rakshasa,' said the goat. 'Their blood is of an excellent flavour and vintage.'

The other goldsmith had been aroused from his sleep, for he had felt a tug at his choti. He heard and saw all that took place that night, and trembled with horror at the discovery that the palace belonged to the terrible rakshasas, people whose natural food was the flesh and blood of man. He got up in a hurry, and on the excuse of making his morning ablutions, left the palace and ran for his life.

The goat learned at once of his flight, and changing herself into a beautiful woman, set off after the goldsmith, crying out plaintively, 'Husband dear, where are you going? Do not leave me behind, I beg of you. Take me with you.' But the goldsmith had caught sight of her feet which were crooked and faced backwards, and he knew that she was the rakshasa woman. He fled as fast as possible, until he reached a great oak tree sacred to the god Shiva. He climbed into its highest branches, and invoked the protection of the god, 'Protect me, O Shiva, lord of spirits and ghosts! Protect me from this terrible rakshasi!'

His prayers must have been heard, because when the rakshasa woman reached the tree, she was unable to climb up after him—it may have been because of her crooked feet—and she sat down beneath it and set up a wail.

'Oh, cruel man,' she complained loudly, 'why have you abandoned me? Do descend, O lord of my life and ravisher of my heart!' She wept and beat her breasts, and the sound of her lamentation rang through the forest.

It so happened that a raja was passing by on a hunting expedition. Seeing a beautiful woman in apparent distress, he went up to console her. And on learning from her the cause of her sorrow, he looked up at the quaking goldsmith and said, 'Fellow, why do you treat your good wife so badly? Come down at once and take her home.'

The goldsmith, who had no intention of descending, replied, 'Your majesty, you are most welcome to my wife. I renounce all claims on her. She is nothing to me.'

Now this raja made a hobby of collecting wives, and he was delighted at the chance of obtaining a beautiful prize so easily. But honour still had to be satisfied.

'We do not accept wives from our subjects, we have to purchase them,' he said. 'Here's five thousand rupees for her. Come down and collect the money.'

'Leave it beneath the tree,' said the prudent goldsmith. 'I have made a vow not to come down so long as she is within sight.'

The raja accordingly left a purse under the tree and, placing the woman in his handsome carriage, took her to his kingdom. And he married her with great pomp and ceremony.

The raja had a favourite horse, a favourite dog, and a favourite son, all of whom he loved very much— but in that order. The first thing the rakshasa queen did was to eat the horse, and throw its bones into the palaces of the other queens.

When the raja discovered that his horse had disappeared, he consulted his new queen, on whom he doted. The wily rakshasa queen said, 'Why don't you look for it in the palaces of the other queens?' The raja instantly set off to visit the other queens— there were seven of them at the time—and found the bones of his favourite horse scattered about their courtyards. In spite of their strong—and for once united—protestations of innocence, the queens were severely rebuked by the raja. He would have had the lot executed had he not been rather vain about having so many wives.

Next day the dog was missing, and the day after, his favourite son. The seven queens were again blamed for their disappearance. The raja was infuriated and decreed that they should all be beheaded. But at the prime minister's intercession, he agreed to spare their lives. Instead he decided to imprison them in a dark cave in the hills for ever. The path to this cave was arduous and labyrinthine, and known only to the raja. The seven queens wailed as one when he blocked the entrance to the cave with a huge boulder and left them in the darkness without any food.

The unfortunate queens would have been forced to eat one another to allay their hunger had not the eldest queen, very fortunately, given birth to a son just when their hunger was becoming unbearable. The ladies unanimously cut the child into seven portions and ate it. A few days later, when another queen gave birth to a child, it suffered the same fate. In this way, six of the queens gave birth to children, all of whom were devoured by the famished queens. But when the seventh and youngest rani gave birth to a son, she refused to do away with it, saying, 'Sisters, I will not kill and eat my son. Here are the six pieces of flesh which you gave me, but which I did not touch. Appease your hunger on them, but let my son live.' And she divided the six pieces amongst the other queens.

When the Lord Shiva, creator and destroyer,

82

saw the young queen's action from his perch on Mount Kailash, he was pleased with her. Descending into the cave in the shape of her father, he said, 'I had heard of your misfortunes, daughter, but could not find any way of communicating with you until now. But henceforth I will see that you receive eight dishes of good food every day, one each for you and your sisters and your child.' Lord Shiva left the cave, and invisible hands supplied the queens with food every day. The virtue of this food was such that within a year, the child grew as tall and strong and intelligent as a youth of twenty—despite always being with seven wailing women. One day he asked his mother, 'Have I no father or uncle or grandfather? And if I do, where are they?'

His mother said, 'You have no father, my son, but your grandfather lives somewhere in the hills. He is a carpenter and supplies us with food.'

'Then bless me and permit me to leave you,' said the prince. 'I will search for my grandfather and see whether we can get you out of this terrible cave.' And that very evening he managed with great difficulty to move the boulder that blocked the mouth of the cave a few inches so that he could squeeze out.

After wandering around in the labyrinthine mazes of the hills for several days, he managed finally to find his grandfather. His grandfather, who had apparently forgiven the raja for imprisoning his daughter in a dark cave with no food, set him on the road to the palace. The prince soon found employment in the palace as a captain of the guard, and he was sent to keep watch over the palace of the rakshasa queen. When the queen looked out of the window to see what the new watchman was like, she recognized the lineaments of the raja in the face of the youth and knew him to be the prince born in the cave. She was angered but also thrilled, for life in the palace had been boring since the departure of her seven rival queens.

That night the rakshasa queen took off her rich clothes and jewels, and artfully dishevelling her hair, retired to the Hall of Anger. Hearing of the queen's fit of depression, the raja followed her into the hall and found her wailing and rolling about on the ground. When the raja entreated her to tell him the cause of her grief, she replied, 'Do you think I have no heart? I have had no news of my father for a year. Send me to my father's palace or send someone to bring me news of his health. Bring me also the singing water and vanaspati rice which grows, fully-cooked, to a height of forty feet. Have these things brought to me soon, or I must leave you. If you love me, send this young guard to fetch them immediately.'

The raja promised most solemnly to do as she directed, and summoning the prince, said, 'My brave young captain, go at once and fetch the singing water, the vanaspati rice and news of the queen's relatives. Hurry, if you value your life, and return as soon as possible. And take this letter from the queen to her father.'

The prince innocently set out for the city of the queen's relatives, who were none other than the rakshasas. He travelled on horseback until he reached the seven hills covered by dense forest. From that point he had to continue on foot.

He had not gone far when he found a tiger in his way. It was a fierce-looking tiger, and as it hadn't killed any game for a day or two, it was in a bad temper. But the prince knew how to deal with this lord of the forest, and stepping up to him, said, 'Good day, uncle, how are you?' For he knew that the secret of survival in the forest is to address a tiger—or any other hostile creature, animal or human—as 'uncle' or 'aunt'; it instantly disarms them.

When the tiger realized the stranger was his nephew, he was a little confused. Greeting the prince gruffly, he moved off into the forest. A little further on, the prince met an elephant, whom he addressed as 'aunt', and a cobra, whom he saluted as 'cousin'. He met a number of wild animals, and by establishing close kinship with all of them, passed unharmed through the forest. On emerging into the foothills, he came across a small thatched hut.

Here the prince found a yogi immersed in a trance. When the yogi opened his eyes, the prince prostrated himself before him and said, 'O wise one, help me in my quest. Tell me where I can find the singing water, the vanaspati rice and the relatives of the queen. Where is the person to whom this letter is addressed?'

The yogi asked the prince to rest with him that night. While the traveller slept, he removed the letter from his coat, and breaking the seal, read it by the light of the dhuni, the perpetual fire which burned before him. The letter went:

Dear Brother,
    As soon as you see the bearer of this letter, kill and devour him.

Your affectionate sister,
The Goat Rakshasi

The yogi burned this letter, and taking up pen, ink and palm leaf paper, wrote the following:

Dear Brother,
    The bearer of this letter is my son. Treat him well, and send through him the singing water and the vanaspati rice.

Your affectionate sister,
The Goat Rakshasi

In the morning, unaware of the change of letters, the prince set out again on his journey. But the yogi warned him that he was now in rakshasa country.

'If you succeed in your enterprise,' advised the yogi, 'do not leave behind a single bone which you may find in the palace, but bring them all away.'

The prince finally reached the palace of the rakshasas—the same palace which had been visited by the seven goldsmiths. The rakshasa chief, on reading his sister's letter, embraced the prince with affection, and introduced him to all his other rakshasa relatives before handing him over to the care of his old mother.

The prince soon gained the confidence of the old lady, and one day he asked her, 'Nani, show me the wonders of this palace. I wish to know the secrets of your life and death. Nani, I love both you and uncle so much that I dread anything bad might happen to you.'

'Do not be afraid on our account,' said the old woman. 'We, the race of rakshasas, bear charmed lives. We fear no death. Come with me, and I will show you what I mean.'

She took the prince into the large Hall of Life where innumerable birds were kept in cages: parrots, peacocks, pigeons, sparrows, woodpeckers, flycatchers and many others.

The old rakshasa woman said, 'Prince, these birds are our lives. As long as they live, we live. When they die, we die. You see, they are protected with great care and cannot be injured by anybody. That myna is my life, that crow is your uncle's, and that peahen is your mother the queen's!'

Then the prince asked, 'Nani, where are the singing water and the vanaspati rice?'

The old woman took him into another room and showed him a bottle of a clear limpid liquid. When she opened the bottle, there flowed out of it the most enchanting music.

'This,' she said, 'is the singing water.' And then taking him into the garden, she showed him a very tall tree and said, 'This is the tree of vanaspati rice.'

The prince was shown other rooms, some of them full of gold and precious stones. He also saw the room in which the bones of all those persons who had been devoured by the rakshasas were kept. Then one day, when the rakshasas had all gone to a neighbour's wedding feast, the prince decided the time to act had come. Entering the Hall of Life, and taking hold of the birds one at a time, he began to kill them by wringing their necks. He did not, however, take the life of the peahen, but took this bird with him.

The bodies of the broken-necked rakshasa people

made a huge pile outside the palace gates. And the prince took the bottle of singing water and a branch of the tree of vanaspati rice, and tying the bones of the dead humans in a bundle, left the palace and in due course reached the hut of the yogi.

The yogi sprinkled some of the singing water on the bones of the victims, and brought them back to life. Amongst them were the six goldsmiths. They rejoiced greatly when they saw the yogi for they recognized the seventh goldsmith. He told them how he had escaped from the clutches of the rakshasa goat, and how he had performed austerities to gain the power to save his friends. The yogi also revealed to the prince the true history of the queen, and suggested that they proceed together to the raja's palace to expose her.

Accompanied by the seven goldsmiths and bearing the singing water, the vanaspati rice and the peahen, the prince entered the forest again. He met his relatives, the tiger, the elephant and the cobra, and each of them presented him with one of their offspring. Then, accompanied by his now-large retinue, he finally entered the raja's city.

Assuming the garb of jugglers, the prince and the goldsmiths went to the Hall of Audience and announced that they would perform a wonderful magic-play called the 'The Rakshasas Unveiled'. The raja and a great assembly gathered to watch the performance. The prince moved fearlessly amongst his strange collection of wild animals, and when he played on a flute, the animals began dancing in a circle round him. He then planted the branch of vanaspati rice, and it immediately grew into a tall tree, and cooked rice of the sweetest flavour rained down upon the spectators, who declared later that they had never tasted anything like it. Then he dug a large tank, and threw the bottle of singing water into it. Music filled the halls of the palace.

The performance lasted several hours, and at the end of it the prince said, 'Now we are going to show you our last and most wonderful act—the dance of the peahen!' He let the bird out of its cage and began to play on his flute.

As soon as the bird began dancing, the rakshasa queen ran out from the audience and began to dance before the whole assembly. The raja was horrified, but he held his peace. Then the prince broke one leg of the peahen, and behold! one leg of the rakshasa queen was broken too. The peahen continued dancing on one leg, and so did the queen. The prince then pulled out one of the bird's wings, and as a result, the queen lost an arm; but the dance continued. Finally the prince broke the neck of the bird, and the queen, uttering a loud shriek, resumed her original shape of a forty-yard-long rakshasi, and fell dead on the spot.

The next scene was still more wonderful. The seven goldsmiths came forward with the seven banished queens—and their sons! The children they had eaten in the cave had been brought back to life by the singing water.

'And so,' concluded Bibiji in her matter-of-fact way, 'everyone lived happily ever after—except for the poor raja who was forced by his ministers to put an end to his hobby of collecting queens.'

the dance continued. Finally the prince broke the neck of the bird, and the queen, uttering a loud shriek, assumed her original shape of a long-tailed ... and fell dead on the spot.

The next scene was still more wonderful. The seven goldsmiths came forward with the seven banished queens—and their sons! The children they had eaten in the cave had been brought back to life by the singing water.

And so concluded Bibhi in her matter-of-fact way, Merren lived happy ever after—except for the poor rajah who was forced by his ministers to put an end to his dislike of collecting queens.

Who Killed the Rani?

ॐ

I

I MET INSPECTOR Keemat Lal a few years ago, when I was living in the hot dusty town of Shahpur in the plains of northern India. My grandfather had owned a house and some land on the outskirts of the town. After his death, this property had been left to me; but as it now had very little value and the town had no attractions for me, I was anxious to sell it. The mild interest that a couple of local property dealers had shown made me decide to remain in Shahpur for a few months.

Keemat Lal was the inspector in charge of the local police station. He was heavily-built, slow and rather ponderous, and inclined to be lazy. But, like most lazy people, he was intelligent. He was also a failure. He had remained an inspector for a number of years, and had given up all hope of further promotion. His luck was against him, he said. He should never have been a policeman. He had been born under the sign of Capricorn, and ought really to have gone into the restaurant business. But it was too late to do anything about it.

The Inspector and I had very little in common. He was about forty-five, and I was thirty. I was a writer of sorts. He seldom read books, and wasn't interested in mine. But, like most rural children, he had been brought up on folk tales and macabre fantasies, and he liked telling a good story as much as he enjoyed hearing one.

Both of us spoke English, and in Shahpur there were not many people who did. In addition, we were both heavy consumers of beer. There were no places of entertainment in the town. The searing heat, the dust that came whirling up from the east, the mosquitoes—as numerous as the flies—and the general monotony, gave one a thirst for something more substantial than stale lemonade.

Shahpur was under partial prohibition, which meant that you could not drink in restaurants or public places, only in the privacy of your own home. This put Keemat Lal in a difficult position. His wife was totally opposed to his imbibing alcohol, and refused to let him bring any into the house.

And, as an inspector of police, it would not have been very wise of him to be seen drinking in the houses of friends or acquaintances, most of whom were local councillors or businessmen, who were frequently involved in litigation. So he turned instead to me—an outsider, a person with no particular attachment to Shahpur, and no involvement in local intrigue.

An added advantage was that my house was on the outskirts of the town, where he would not be disturbed easily. Two or three evenings each week, just as the sun was going down and making it possible for one to emerge from the khas-cooled confines of a dark high-ceilinged bedroom, he would appear on my veranda steps, mopping the sweat from his face with a small towel which he used instead of a handkerchief. And I, having bathed for the second time that day, would get into a clean shirt and join him on the veranda. My only servant, excited at the prospect of serving an inspector of police, would hurry out with glasses, a bucket of ice and several bottles of Golden Eagle beer.

One evening, when he had overtaken a fourth Golden Eagle, I said, 'You must have had some interesting cases in your career, Inspector.'

'Most of them were dull ones, Mr Bond,' he said. 'My successful cases were dull. The sensational ones went unsolved—otherwise I might have been a superintendent by now. I suppose you are talking of murder cases, being a writer. Do you remember the shooting of the minister of the interior? I was on that one, but it was a political murder, and we never solved it.'

'Tell me about a case you solved,' I said. 'An interesting one.' And when I saw him looking uncomfortable, I added, 'You don't have to worry, Inspector, I'm a very discreet person—in spite of all the beer I consume.'

'But how can you be discreet? You are a writer.'

I protested against this. 'Writers are usually very discreet. They always change the names of people and places.'

He smiled sardonically. 'And how would you describe me, if you were to put me into a book?'

'Oh, I'd leave you as you are,' I said. 'No one would believe in you anyway.'

He laughed indulgently and poured out more beer. 'I suppose I can change names too . . . I will tell you about a very interesting case. The victim was an unusual person, and so was the murderer. It is usually the nature or character of the victim that brings about his or her demise. The murderers are often colourless individuals, driven by greed, jealousy or revenge. But you must promise not to repeat the story to anyone.'

'I promise,' I lied.

'Do you know Mussoorie?'

'The hill station? Yes, I lived there as a boy. I remember the place quite well.'

'Good. This happened about three years ago, shortly after I had been stationed at Mussoorie.'

He took about two hours to tell me about the case, speaking in a rather blurred, hesitant voice. We finished a great deal of beer. I thought it was an interesting story—particularly because it threw considerable light on Keemat Lal's own character.

II

Inspector Keemat Lal was off duty. That meant he was comfortably ensconced in the bar of the Himalaya Hotel, musing over the evening's first brandy-and-water. He felt it would take at least three brandies to banish the irritability that had been growing in him all day. His application for a transfer had been turned down. He had given up hoping for a promotion, but he felt that his superiors at the divisonal headquarters might at least have had the heart to post him to a district where something happened. It was true he had been in Mussoorie for only three months; but three months in a fair-sized town in the plains would have seen him investigating at least three murders, a dozen dacoities, several cases of assault, and a good deal of 420. This last misdemeanour—cheating and swindling in their many forms—was popularly known as '420', which was the section number of the Indian penal code which dealt with such crimes.

But in this quaint little hill resort—six thousand feet above sea level—there had been, in the space of three months, no murders, no dacoities, no cases of assault, and an insignificant amount of 420.

There had been a couple of thefts. In the most exciting case, the thief had turned out to be an itinerant hippie who had taken a fancy to the Victorian chamber pots still found in old Mussoorie houses. He had taken to pilfering them and selling them at a profit to an antique dealer from Delhi.

And then there had been the book-thief. Keemat Lal had almost forgotten him. Of course that had been before his arrival, and there was nothing that could be done about it. A bookish visitor had joined the very old and much-neglected local library which had a membership of fifteen persons who seldom used it. The book collector, when he left Mussoorie, decamped with over a hundred library books. Everyone wondered why he would have bothered to take away so much unread—and surely worthless—books. But later, the municipality was startled out of its monsoonal lethargy when it transpired that the collector had made a small fortune by selling first editions of *Plain Tales from the Hills* and *Memoirs of Fanny Hill*, an early pirated edition of Tennyson's poems and other literary treasures at a London auction. They sent for a bibliophile to value the remaining books, but of course the collector had taken everything of value.

Keemat Lal emptied his glass and called for another brandy. While a waiter was fetching it, the Inspector looked out of the windows with distaste. It was drizzling, and a strong wind whipped the rain against the windowpanes. Though it was mid-February, too late for more snow, the weather was still very cold, and Keemat Lal had not taken off his muffler and woollen gloves. The hotel's 'Canadian stove' gave out plenty of warmth. At home there would be only a charcoal brazier at which to warm his hands—and no brandy to comfort his stomach. His wife did not approve of alcohol even at high altitudes.

He was about to start his second brandy when he noticed the steward hurrying across the empty lounge towards his table. He had a premonition of impending doom; but it passed, leaving only a sense of irritation. There was no one else in the room—Mussoorie did not get visitors before April—and he knew he was going to be disturbed.

'Excuse me for bothering you, sir,' said the young steward. 'There is a man outside who wants to see you.'

'Have you told him I am here?' asked Keemat Lal grimly.

'He seemed to know you would be here, sir.'

'Why don't you tell him to go to hell?' suggested the Inspector.

'I have already done so, sir. But he won't go. Something seems to have happened at the Rani's house.'

'The Rani's house? I didn't know there were any ranis left in Mussoorie.'

'Everyone knows this one, sir.'

'Her chamberpots are probably missing. Tell the man we've found the culprit, and the Rani will soon get her commodes back.'

'I think it's something more serious, sir. The man is babbling about blood and murder. I can't follow his dialect very well, but he appears to be quite frightened.'

Keemat Lal sighed, looked sadly at his brandy, and swallowed it in one gulp. Then he got up slowly, rather painfully—he was a tall portly man his paunch swelling out over his belt—and walked heavily towards the hotel entrance.

An icy blast from the door almost knocked the small woollen cap off his head. 'Well, what is it?' he said angrily, glaring at the swarthy, rather wild-looking man who stood shivering in the porch.

'Salaam Inspector sahib. May the gods forgive me for disturbing you at this hour, but something terrible has happened. The Rani is dead. I saw her with my own eyes, when I took her the flour and sugar she had asked me to buy.'

Keemat Lal looked at him disbelievingly. Sudden death was not in keeping with the atmosphere of Mussoorie. 'Are you sure she is dead?'

'As surely as I know I am alive, sahib. Her head is cut open, and there is blood everywhere.'

Keemat Lal did not stand irresolute for long.

'How far is the Rani's house?'

'About half a mile.'

'Come along, then. You can tell me everything on the way. Why did you kill her?'

The man stood petrified. His lips moved soundlessly and his eyes darkened with fear.

'Oh, never mind,' said Keemat Lal, seeing that the man was ready to faint in his arms. 'Of course you did not do it. Let us get a move on. What is your name?'

'Chotte Lal, sahib. I swear I did not kill the Rani.'

They had to walk the distance. The roads in this remote area were not suitable for vehicles. There was a bicycle at the police station, but it was possible to ride it only along the level stretch of the main road, known in every hill station as 'the Mall'. He could have obtained a pony of course, but it was doubtful if one of the local ponies would have got the Inspector to his destination in good time. He did not get along well with ponies. On first coming to Mussoorie, he had sat on one and had gone jogging along the Mall at a brisk trot. The people in the bazaar had smiled tolerantly, but the children had not bothered to conceal their amusement. They cheered him down the road. And he had overheard a remark made by one urchin to another—'Have you seen a melon on horseback before?'

Now, sharing an umbrella with his nervous informer, Keemat Lal reached the small ill-lit police station. There were two contables on night duty— Sant Ram and Govind Singh, both hill men who had joined the police force when their small terraced fields could not produce enough to support their families. Govind Singh was already in his cot, rolled up in a blanket. Sant Ram, a tall cadaverous man in his late twenties, was in uniform, watching over a boiling kettle.

'Ah, Inspector sahib!' he called out. 'Please come and have a cup of tea!' Given a plentiful supply of tea, Sant Ram had nothing to complain about.

'Later, perhaps,' said Keemat Lal, who was not a tea-addict. 'But just now I need you. Something is up at the Rani's house. Get your umbrella and come along.'

'Yes, sir,' said Sant Ram giving his kettle a sad lingering look. He wished the Inspector sahib could wait until they had both had some tea. What was the hurry? No one hurried in Mussoorie. Even dead people could be burnt or buried at leisure, especially in the winter months. And a glass of hot sweet tea always increased one's efficiency. Six glasses of strong tea were Sant Ram's daily minimum.

But the Inspector was waiting for him in the rain and he would have to go along . . .

Keemat Lal made another stop on the way, this time at Dr Gulati's clinic. Dr Gulati usually performed post-mortems for the police. He finished writing a prescription for one of his regular patients, and was soon ready to accompany the Inspector. He was a stout man, but he had lived in Mussoorie for a number of years, often walking to see patients who lived three or four miles away, and he set a brisk pace for Keemat Lal.

The four men set off down a dark stony path to the Rani's house. A strong wind had sprung up, which drove the rain into their faces.

'How did she die?' asked Dr Gulati. He had retired—rather suddenly—from the Army Medical Corps some five years ago.

'That's for us to find out,' said the Inspector. 'I will not be surprised if we find her alive. This man says he found her lying on the floor with her head cut open.'

Dr Gulati drew back his coat sleeve and looked at his watch. It was almost nine o'clock. He yawned and said, 'I hope she's alive and unhurt. I have some guests coming over for dinner.'

'Yes, it's a nuisance,' said Keemat Lal. 'But you don't seem surprised, doctor. Did the Rani have enemies?'

'I don't know about enemies. But she was not popular.'

'You were her doctor?'

'I was, at one time. But she changed her doctors frequently. She was a difficult woman to please. If I did not give her the disease she wanted to have, she would be most offended. Her heart was always healthy, but she told everyone it was weak.'

'Well, these princely families were always a spoilt lot,' observed Keemat Lal.

'Oh, she was not really a rani of any of the former states, although she called herself one. She was related to some royal family or other, but she had very little money. Her husband left her for another woman about eight years ago. When he died, his money and property went to his second wife.'

'It is beginning to sound complicated,' said Keemat Lal.

They were nearing the house. It had been a fine house once, you could see that. It was one of the houses built over a hundred years ago when the hill stations were first becoming fashionable. The Rani had not bothered to keep it in repair. The roof unpainted and held down in places by large stones. Plaster was peeling off the walls. Even in the dim light of the street lamp, there was no mistaking its sorry condition. The wrought iron gate creaked on its hinges when Keemat Lal pushed it open. The front door was half-open, and a light was burning in the room.

'Was the light on when you found her?' asked Keemat Lal.

'No, sahib,' said Chotte. 'I switched it on myself.'

'You went in without calling or knocking?'

'I called twice, but there was no answer. The Rani often left the door open for me.'

Keemat Lal opened the door very gently, and stood in the doorway. The electric bulb was weak, leaving the corners of the room in darkness. But the dead woman—it was obvious to the Inspector that she was dead—lay on the bare floor directly beneath the light. She wore a purple sari. One of her slippers had come off and lay near the door. There was a deep diagonal wound across her left temple. Blood had flowed from it fairly copiously, trickling into a corner of the room where a small nondescript dog was now sniffing at it. Keemat Lal shooed the dog away. Tail between its legs, it slunk out of the room into the veranda.

The Inspector and Dr Gulati stood over the body, while Constable Sant Ram and Chotte Lal remained at the door.

'I suppose it *is* the Rani', said Keemat Lal to no one in particular.

'Oh, yes,' said Dr Gulati, going down on one knee to examine her. 'There's no mistaking her . . .'

She had been a woman of about fifty. She was dark-complexioned, and had high cheekbones, a broad nose with flaring nostrils and a rather wide mouth. Though she could never have been a beautiful woman, Keemat Lal felt that she must have been attractive in some indefinable way. Her large eyes were wide open, staring up at the ceiling.

The frozen expression on her face was one of anger, not of fear. Keemat Lal found this unusual. He had seldom seen anger on a dead person's face. Occasionally he had seen fear; but usually dead faces were quite expressionless.

'She was struck across the head with something sharp and heavy,' said Dr Gulati. 'It must have been something like an axe—probably a small light axe, otherwise the injury would have been larger.'

'Could it have been a kukri or a sickle?'

'No, I don't think it was a curved blade. The wound would have been longer and probably not so deep.'

'Well, whoever did it took the axe with him. Would it have required much strength to inflict a fatal blow?'

'Not necessarily. Not if there had been a lot of momentum behind the blow. A woman could have done it, if that's what you're thinking.'

'Can you fix the time of death, doctor?'

'Not exactly. She has been dead three or four hours, I should say. That means she was killed some time between four and six in the evening. That's a cautious estimate, Inspector.'

'For an ex-army doctor, you are much too cautious,' said Keemat Lal with a chuckle. He swung around to the shivering servant. 'At what time did you find her?' he snapped.

'It was about six o'clock, sahib. I know, because I passed the clock tower in the bazaar at fifteen minutes to six, and it takes less than fifteen minutes to reach the house.'

'And where were you before that?'

'In the bazaar, sahib, buying vegetables and flour for the Rani.'

'And when did you last see her—I mean, before you found her dead?'

'In the morning, sahib.'

'Did you notice anything then? Did she seem worried, was she afraid of anything?'

'She was always worried, sahib. She was never afraid. Others were afraid of her.'

The doctor permitted himself a smile. 'He is right, you know. She was the worrying kind. Nervous, irritable and highly-strung. She also had a very bad temper. And when she lost it, she lost all her nervousness.'

Keemat Lal was unwilling to give Chotte any respite. It was a rule with him to look upon the first man on the scene of the crime as the most likely suspect. In five cases out of ten, this surmise proved correct. The Rani, according to the doctor, had not been wealthy; but Keemat Lal felt she must have had something of value.

110

'What's your name?' he asked again. He was not very good at remembering names.

Chotte Lal repeated his name.

'Note it down,' said the Inspector to Constable Sant Ram, and Sant Ram, with a sudden display of energy, produced a notebook from his pocket. But he had forgotten his pencil. Looking around helplessly, he spotted one lying on the dead woman's desk, picked it up gratefully, and took down Chotte's name. The doctor had meanwhile finished his examination.

'How much did the Rani pay you?' asked Keemat Lal of the servant.

'Nothing,' said Chotte.

'Note it down,' said Keemat Lal to Sant Ram. And then, to Chotte, 'Do you mean you worked for her for nothing?'

'Only in my free hours, sahib. The Rani was very good to me once'—the doctor raised his eyebrows in surprise—'I work as a peon in the bank. The Rani got the job for me two years ago.'

'I see,' said Keemat Lal. The Rani must have had some influence to get him the job. 'Note it down,' said Keemat Lal to his constable. 'Note it down.'

'I have already done so, sir.'

'Good. Very good. Keep this man in custody. I

will want to question him at the station.'

'Sahib, my children are waiting for me,' said Chotte.

'They have a mother, haven't they?'

Chotte hung his head. 'Their mother is dead, sahib. And my mother is very old and cannot manage them on her own.'

'Oh, well,' said Keemat Lal. 'We shall see. We will not keep you all night—unless, of course, you happened to have killed the Rani.'

'I, sahib! She was my mother and my sister and my father!' Catching the doctor's eye, he added, 'It is true, she was rough and rude in her ways, and there were some who did not like her, but at heart she was very good . . . I would rather my own life had been taken!'

Keemat Lal gave Chotte a wry smile. 'I hope you are right, my friend. And now, to demonstrate your devotion, come and help us carry the Rani to her bed. We cannot leave her on the floor all night.'

Chotte, after some slight hesitation, took the corpse by the feet. The Inspector and the doctor took the arms. Together they lifted the body and carried it into an adjoining room, where they laid it out on a bed. Keemat Lal noticed that there was very little furniture in any of the rooms. Even the bed was hard, covered by only two blankets.

'The Rani lived a simple life,' he observed. 'No comforts at all.'

'I told you, she had very little money,' said Dr Gulati.

'The why the devil did anyone bother to kill her?' asked Keemat Lal resentfully.

III

He was still asking himself this question the following morning while he walked thoughtfully back to the Rani's house. He knew that money was the motivation for most murders, but the Rani apparently had none. The previous night, while searching the house, he had found a few hundred rupees in a desk drawer. The Rani's jewel box contained nothing of great value, nor was there any sign of anyone having tampered with it. Nothing in the rooms seemed to have been disturbed by an intruder. The motive then must have been a deeply personal one—jealousy, revenge, blackmail, perhaps a fit of madness . . . Or had she known too much about someone? The thing to do was to see and question the Rani's close associates—her friends, neighbours and servants, if she had any. There was some correspondence of hers to go through, but Keemat Lal put off reading this. He did not enjoy reading other people's letters; they usually depressed him

As he neared the rise in the path which led to the Rani's gate, he found the way blocked by a group of children playing cricket. When they saw him, they moved aside to let him pass, and gazed after him with undisguised curiosity. Three were boys, the fourth in the group was a girl. She was not really playing with them, only watching the game a little condescendingly. She must have been thirteen or fourteen. She was a dark girl, with her hair done in a pigtail. She was as rough and vociferous as the boys, and her clothes were torn and rather dirty. Keemat Lal liked her features: her large expressive eyes and her well-shaped nose and mouth. He gave her one of the smiles which he usually reserved for his own infant son. She did not respond to the smile and stared at the Inspector with what he sensed was mild hostility.

He was a little out of breath by the time he reached the Rani's gate. The body had been removed earlier that morning. Constable Sant Ram now sat on a stone bench, chewing a roll of paan. He spat the red juice into the flower bed. Chotte Lal, who had been temporarily released from police custody—several shopkeepers declared having seen him in the bazaar between four and six the previous evening—now showed his gratitude by mopping up the bloodstains from the floor. He did this without a tremor, as though the blood were a goat's or a chicken's. He was not a man with much imagination. Blood divorced from body had no meaning for him. Finally, Keemat Lal told him he could go home.

It was nine o'clock, and the sun came over the oaks and deodars, through the windows of the Rani's front room. Keemat Lal went to the desk, pulled out a bundle of letters, and sifted through them. Some of them were reminders for unpaid bills, thus confirming Dr Gulati's opinion that the Rani was in financial difficulties. There was a short letter from someone who might have been a relative, asking the Rani the reason for her long silence. This was about six months old and bore a Delhi address. Keemat Lal told Sant Ram to take note of the address. There were no letters of a very personal nature. Either the Rani did not have friends or she did not correspond with them. But there was a note—a recent one—from someone called Joan Simmons, asking the Rani to tea on Tuesday. That must have been last Tuesday, three days ago. Glancing at the address, Keemat Lal discovered that Joan Simmons lived in the next house, just thirty yards up the hill. He looked out of the window, and saw a well-kept cottage perched on the spur of a hill directly overlooking the Rani's house. Well; it was a start. Joan Simmons, whoever she was, ought to be able to tell him something about the Rani.

Just then the telephone rang.

Keemat Lal gave a start. He had not been aware that there was a telephone in the room. Glancing around distractedly, he saw it standing on a low stool in a dark corner. Reflecting that the Rani must have paid her telephone bills at least, he went down on his haunches and picked up the receiver. The person at the other end started speaking before Keemat could say his habitual gruff 'Hallo'.

'Listen, my dear Nita. Can you come and see me this afternoon? I am a little worried about what happened yesterday.'

It was a man's voice, deep and strong. Keemat Lal held his breath, hoping that this mysterious caller would continue talking. But in trying to squat down more comfortably, he lost his balance and came down painfully on his rear. His knee banged against the stool, and the telephone fell over. When Keemat held the receiver to his ear again, there was only a purring sound. He had been disconnected. He got up from the floor, cursing his own bulk, and then waited hopefully for the telephone to ring again. But there was no second call.

Keemat Lal wondered who the caller could have been. The man hadn't said much, and yet he had said quite a lot. He had obviously meant to speak to the Rani—he could not yet have learnt of her death—and the expression 'my dear Nita' suggested that he was on familiar terms with her. And what was he worried about? Something that had happened yesterday. There were some three hundred telephone subscribers in Mussoorie, and Keemat Lal did not intend phoning each of them in the hope of recognizing a voice. Besides, the man might have phoned from a restaurant or the post office. Keemat felt that he had lost an opportunity to identify one of the Rani's more intimate acquaintances.

He wondered what he should do next; then he saw the note from Joan Simmons, and remembered that he was going to see the lady. Joan, he knew, was a girl's name. As a boy, he had gone to a convent school, and he distinctly remembered a girl called Joan—a twelve-year-old Anglo-Indian with the most beautiful, wicked eyes . . . Brushing the dust from his clothes, he left the Rani's house.

When he reached the gate, he found that the children had gone. But there was a dog—the mongrel that he had found in the Rani's room the previous night—examining the spilled-over contents of a dustbin.

'Sant Ram,' said the Inspector to his betel-chewing constable.

'Sir?'

117

'Do you see that dog?'

'Yes, sir,' said Sant Ram, giving the dog a hostile look.

'Did it belong to the Rani?'

'I do not think so, sir. Ranis only keep imported dogs.'

'Don't be a fool. Go and find out whose dog it is. Ask in the nearest bania shop. Ask any servants who work around here.'

Sant Ram got up from the bench with alacrity. There was small bania's shop just round the corner, where he knew he would be offered a cup of tea. And someone there would be sure to know about the dog.

'And meet me here after half an hour,' said Keemat Lal.

Time enough for two glasses of tea! Constable Sant Ram saluted smartly, and set off for the shop. Inspector Keemat Lal hitched his trousers up a little, and braced himself for another stiff climb.

IV

In front of the Simmonses' house, a peach tree had just burst into pale pink blossom. The garden had been raked and manured for a spring sowing, and the spear-like leaves of iris were shooting up at the borders. As Keemat Lal walked in at the open gate, he heard voices raised in song—a man's and a woman's—and as he approached the front door, he was able to recognize the words.

He rather liked the tune, and began humming it to himself; but then he realized its import, and lost his enthusiasm. Missionaries!

Keemat Lal quailed at the thought of interviewing foreign missionaries. They always made him feel ill-at-ease. The gentle patronizing way they had of looking at one, of summing one up behind a mask of politeness, of considering one's possibilities . . . Well, he had a job to do and he was not going to be intimidated by the religious-minded, whatever their denomination. His wife was a devout Hindu, but he was something of an agnostic himself. You could have described Keemat Lal as a god-fearing atheist.

He knocked on the front door. No one seemed to have heard him. The singing continued, louder than before. Keemat Lal knocked more forcefully, bruising his knuckles in the process. Then he noticed a bell push to his right and, feeling foolish, pressed it ferociously. The singing ceased. A few bars were played out on a piano, and then there was complete silence.

The door was opened by a short, chubby, pink-faced man who wore spectacles. He must have been about thirty-five. He beamed at the Inspector.

119

'Good morning,' he said in a light musical voice. 'And what can I do for you?' And then, as an afterthought, he added, 'Oh, you must be the man who's come to fix the taps.'

Keemat Lal regretted not having worn his uniform that morning. But he puffed himself up and, trying to sound dignified but not offended, said, 'I am Inspector Lal, Indian Police Service.'

'Oh yes, of course,' said Mr Simmons, beaming even more profusely. 'Do come in. I suppose it's that dreadful business about the Rani.'

Keemat Lal couldn't quite place the man's nationality. His accent wasn't nasal enough to be American, and at the same time, it wasn't the conventional English accent.

'You know about the murder?' asked Keemat.

'Who doesn't? In a small place like Mussoorie, news travels fast, even if nothing else does . . . I hear you've arrested the servant.'

'No one has been arrested as yet, Mr . . . Simmons? Yes. The servant was held for questioning but he is now at liberty.'

Mr Simmons guided Keemat Lal into a small sitting room, brightly-curtained, neat and antiseptic. Mrs Simmons came forward to receive the Inspector.

'This is Inspector Lal,' said Mr Simmons with the cheery air of a cleric introducing a new member of his congregation. 'He's come about Nita.'

'I'm so glad you are going to do something about it,' said Joan Simmons, flashing a brilliant smile at the Inspector.

Keemat Lal felt himself going a little weak at the knees. This always happened—so he told me later—when he met someone who was decidedly sexy. And at the time he thought, 'If this woman is a missionary, she won't have any difficulty finding converts!'

She couldn't have been more than twenty-five. She had straw-coloured hair, eyes the blue of a Siamese kitten's, and the fresh healthy glow of an Anglo-Saxon girl who has not lived very long in the east.

But she was American. Keemat Lal knew this from her accent when she said with a smile, 'We didn't do it, Mr Lal,' and he forced himself to join in their laughter. She pronounced Lal as in 'pal'.

When Keemat Lal had taken a chair and the banter subsided, there were a few moments of awkward silence. Then Mr Simmons—who was in fact English, from the Isle of Man—had an inspiration. 'Would you care for some tea, Inspector?'

'No, thank you.'

'Coffee?' asked Joan Simmons.

Keemat Lal hesitated, almost said yes, and then decided it would be weakness on his part to accept any hospitality in the course of his investigations. 'Some other time, thank you,' he said. 'I just wanted to make some enquiries, you understand. The Rani was known to you?'

'We were friendly neighbours,' said Simmons non-commitally. 'We saw her quite often, but I can't say we knew her. She came up to see us sometimes and she talked a lot about other people, but she never said much about herself—not that we were inquisitive, you know . . .'

'Oh, I wouldn't put it like that, John,' said Mrs Simmons. 'As missionaries, Inspector, we are deeply concerned with a person's way of life, past and future. But we did not want Nita—the Rani—to feel that we were either curious or censorious. So we did not ask her too many questions. We had of course heard this and that . . .'

'Yes?' prompted Keemat.

Joan Simmons hesitated, her blue eyes a little doubtful. 'Well, they were just rumours. A small place like Mussoorie would perish of boredom if it wasn't for gossip and rumour. We're newcomers, Mr Lal, and there isn't much we can tell you. I think you'll learn more from old Miss Bean or from Mrs Kapoor—although neither of them liked the Rani very much.'

'Did you like her?' asked Keemat.

'We try not to dislike people,' said Simmons a little unctuously. 'The Rani was not a popular person. She was quarrelsome and aggressive. Some people said she had the evil eye. But I think her loneliness and many disappointments were at the bottom of it. Wouldn't you say so, Joan?'

'I would. She was a very unhappy woman. This was not apparent right away, but you could sense it.'

'Do you know why her husband left her?' asked Keemat.

Again Joan Simmons hesitated. She looked away and said, 'It was because of another woman—or so we were told.'

'Yes, it was many years ago. The husband is dead. Do you know if the second wife ever visited the Rani?'

'I really wouldn't know, Mr Lal. As I said, we haven't been here very long. But we hope to stay for some time. These hills are lovely—especially during the rains when everyone goes away.' In an oblique and charming way, she was critical of things Indian. Most people missed the innuendoes. Keemat Lal sensed them. He would have resented them in a man, but in a woman they could be forgiven!

He was silent for a minute or two, fiddling with the gold signet ring on his little finger. 'Just for my own satisfaction,' he said with circumspection, 'can you tell me where you were yesterday evening—both of you?'

'Right here, at home,' said Simmons. 'Miss Bean came over for tea. She's English—an old lady who lives alone. The only survivor of what was once a large family.'

'And when did you have tea?'

'Four o'clock sharp. That's Miss Bean's teatime, and she wouldn't like it if we made her wait till later,' Simmons smiled benevolently. 'I think you can cross her off your list of suspects, Inspector. Miss Bean is eighty-four, she couldn't and wouldn't hurt a fly.'

'Oh, it was your own movements I was thinking of,' said Keemat with a smile. 'Still, I would like to see Miss Bean. If she came to tea at four o'clock, she may have seen someone when she passed the Rani's house. Where does she live?'

'About a hundreds yards down the hill. You won't be able to see the cottage from here because of the oak trees.'

'And when did she leave your place?'

'After about an hour and a half.'

'So she could have seen someone on her way

back. Did you and Mrs Simmons stay at home after your guest left?'

'Oh yes,' said Simmons.

'Not entirely,' said his wife. 'We saw Miss Bean down the difficult part of the slope, as far as the Rani's gate. Then we stopped for a few minutes at the bania's shop to buy some of that hot stuff—I can't stand it myself but John loves it—and then we came back up again. We were out for about fifteen minutes—which must put us on your list of suspects, Mr Lal!'

Keemat Lal waved one hand in a deprecatory manner, but he did not deny the supposition. Mr Simmons urged him to have a cup of tea, and his wife repeated the offer of coffee, but Keemat remarked that he was very busy and that it was almost eleven o'clock. They moved out into the garden. Some winter jasmine, its butter-yellow flowers sprinkling the hillside, attracted their attention. At that time of the year, it was the only spot of colour in the garden. Keemat, with an effort, stooped to see if the flowers had any scent, and noticed that from the edge of the garden one could get a good view of the Rani's gate and front veranda. He straightened up and let his gaze wander down the path. Constable Sant Ram was leaning against a wall, scratching himself indulgently.

'Yesterday evening, when you got back to the house,' said Keemat, 'did you spend any time out here, or did you go straight in?'

Simmons pondered the question for a few moments before answering. 'Joan went in, but I think I pottered about a little.'

'You were out here a little while?' Keemat sounded enthusiastic. 'Did you look down the path? Did you see anyone entering or leaving the Rani's house, or hanging around near the gate?'

Simmons tried hard to remember. 'I must have looked down once or twice. I think there were some children playing in the road, but they are often there, and I can't be sure of the time. Wait a minute, though, there *was* someone. The butcher! Yes, he was at the front door. He had a basket of meat with him, and he was having an argument with the Rani.'

'Was it a very heated argument?'

'The Rani was shouting a lot. But then she always does—I mean, did. I wouldn't attach too much importance to it, Inspector. The Rani was frequently quarrelling with tradesmen and menials. I think it gave her enjoyment to wield some of her old authority. I believe she had been very wealthy once, with a large retinue of servants.'

'Still, I must see the butcher. Do you know where he lives?'

'Just carry on up the path,' said Simmons. 'He stays with his family in some broken-down quarters.'

Keemat Lal sighed. Another uphill climb! These roads were too steep and narrow for even a jeep. He looked at his watch again: it was past eleven, and he was getting hungry. But he did not think he would enjoy his lunch if he did not first see the butcher. He thanked the couple for their help, bestowing a kindly protective smile on Joan Simmons. Whatever happened, his smile seemed to promise, she need have no fears from any killer. He, Keemat Lal, would see to that!

He was met outside the gate by Constable Sant Ram.

'I have found out about the dog, sir.'

'What dog? Oh, the dog, yes!' He had almost forgotten the dog—he had been thinking about Mrs Simmons. 'Well, what about it?'

'It belongs to the bania's daughter. The girl who was playing in the road. The Rani gave it to her a few months ago.'

V

Keemat Lal remembered the girl in the road. He did not usually have a good memory for children, and so he was surprised at himself for remembering the girl so distinctly. If the dog had been given to her

127

by the Rani, it would naturally find its way back to its previous owner's house from time to time. He would speak to the girl. She seemed an odd little creature, and might be able to help him.

He paused in his ascent of the slope, and wiped his brow. He found the sun surprisingly warm for February—or was it that he was accumulating more surplus flesh? Sant Ram was already at the top of the slope, waiting for his chief to catch up. The impertinence of the man!

'You wait outside,' said Keemat, who sometimes felt self-conscious in his constable's presence. 'I don't want to alarm the butcher.' He felt the excuse was somewhat lame, but could not think of a better one. No one could possibly have been alarmed to see Sant Ram, who would do almost any favour in exchange for a glass of tea—unlike more hardened policemen who might have expected something more substantial.

The butcher was still out on his rounds, but his wife—a broad fair woman with great spreading hips like the trunk of a banyan tree—offered to send her small son after him. Keemat Lal said he would wait, and the boy, half-naked but oblivious to the cold, scampered up the hillside in search of his father.

The butcher's wife did not offer the Inspector a

seat, because she knew he would not take it. His prestige would suffer. Instead he paced up and down the yard, his progress continually interrupted by a rooster and a number of cackling hens.

Sitting in the sun on a string charpoy was a young woman in her early twenties. She was stitching some cotton garments. Keemat Lal could not help noticing her. She was exquisitely fair and her cheeks were pink, and she had that rare northern beauty which one reads about in fairy tales or Urdu poetry. And Keemat, who was very rarely poetic, murmured a couplet from Hafiz:

'Look not upon the dimple of her chin,
Danger lurks there! . . .'

He was amazed to hear the butcher's wife addressing the young woman as 'sister'—to be precise, 'sister-in-law'. Keemat could see little resemblance between the butcher—whom he had often seen—and this beautiful young creature. The butcher was a rough sullen man of unprepossessing appearance. But then, he drank heavily, mostly raw country liquor. No man, reflected Keemat glancing down at the curve of his paunch, could keep his youthful good looks on a steady diet of beer or rice-wine—or even the best of Indian brandies.

The girl stared back at Keemat with an impassive

expression. And then Bishan Singh, the butcher, arrived, a basket on his head, his son at his heels.

'Namaste, Inspector sahib,' he said. 'Had I known you wanted some meat, I would have brought it to your house. You should not have taken the trouble to walk so far.'

He set his basket down, and produced a leg of pork from a folded cloth. But Keemat was more interested in the meat chopper that lay across the basket, its long sharp blade glistening in the sun. He stooped, took the chopper by the handle, and examined it closely. The butcher looked at him with an expression that was a mixture of amusement and alarm. The chopper had been used recently, there were pieces of meat still clinging to the blade. Keemat expected that it had been washed and used several times since the previous evening.

'Let me see you cut some meat,' he said.

'Do yo want a kilo of pork, sahib, or two? And do you like the fatty bits?'

'I don't eat pork, you fool. I want to see you use the chopper, that's all.'

'But I cannot spoil my meat, sahib, if you are not going to take any of it. Others may not want the piece I cut.'

Keemat Lal threw the chopper back into the basket. 'Your behaviour is very suspicious, my friend. Do you know that the Rani was killed yesterday evening?'

'No, sahib. This is the first I have heard of it.' The man seemed genuinely surprised—but not distressed.

'The whole town knows of it,' said Keemat impatiently. 'Do you mean to tell me you haven't heard anything?'

'I had only just gone out, sahib. No doubt I would have heard about it before long.'

'The Rani was killed at six o'clock yesterday evening. And that's the time you were in her house.'

'I was not in her house, Inspector Sahib.'

'Don't lie to me. You were seen talking to the Rani, quarrelling with her!'

'I was talking to the Rani, but I was not in her house.'

'Where were you, then?'

'Outside, in the garden. I have never entered the Rani's house.'

'All right, all right, you did not go in. But you were there at six o'clock, or just before.'

'No, sahib, it must have been at about four o'clock. At six o'clock, I was at the Bean miss-sahib's house.'

'You are lying again! Miss Bean could not have reached her home so soon—she had been having tea at the missionaries' house.'

'True, sahib. I was waiting for her when she came home. I do not know what time it was, but she bought a kilo of pork from me and ordered some sausages. Why don't you ask her?'

Keemat Lal felt nonplussed. The man seemed so self-assured, so confident—and if Miss Bean confirmed his statement, what was to be made of Mr Simmons's assertion that he had seen the butcher at the Rani's house after the old lady had set off down the hill for her cottage? Was it possible that the missionary was lying?

Well, he would try another approach. He had before him a likely suspect, and he was not going to let him off so easily. But the number of people involved in the Rani's affairs appeared to be increasing. That bothered him. He wished he had something in hand—something concrete—for instance, the weapon . . .

'All right,' he persisted, 'you were with the Rani some time yesterday evening?'

'True, sahib.'

'And you were quarrelling with her?'

The butcher, for once, did not have a ready reply. His eyes refused to meet the Inspector's and he turned his head away.

'You were quarrelling with her,' continued

Keemat relentlessly. 'You were shouting at each other loud enough to be heard all over the hillside. Come on, Bishan Singh, what was it all about? Someone else will tell me, if you don't. Was it the price of the pork? Its quality? Did she refuse to pay? Surely you would not threaten a woman over such trivialities?'

During all this questioning, Bishan Singh had been squatting on the ground beside his basket. Now he stood up. 'I did not threaten anyone, sahib.'

'Then the Rani was threatening you, right?'

'Yes, she was threatening me.'

'Why?'

'You would not believe me if I told you the truth.'

'I can believe anything, my friend. Even the truth.'

Bishan Singh glanced swiftly at his wife, who shook her head, and then at his sister, whose face remained impassive. 'She wanted me to do something for her. It was about my sister.'

'Oh?' Keemat was not expecting this.

'Yes. You see, sahib, the Rani had a friend, Mr Dalip Singh. He is a wealthy man. You must know him. He has property all over Mussoorie. He has a wife and two children as well, but he is not satisfied with that! He has a weakness for women—they are his hobby—and he pays generously for his pleasures. You may not believe me, Inspector sahib, but I tell you, the Rani acted on his behalf. She found girls for him. He does not mind if they are low-caste or poor, as long as they are young and good-looking— the younger the better. He rewarded the Rani well for her efforts.'

Keemat Lal was dumbfounded. His mouth fell open, and he goggled like a goldfish. 'Do you mean to tell me . . .'

'I am a poor man, sahib,' continued Bishan Singh, determined to have his say. 'But there is such a thing as honour, and even a butcher's family may be honourable. My sister is already engaged to be married. And even if she was not, I would never agree to her providing amusement for Dalip Singh or anyone else. No matter how profitable.'

'Do you mean . . .' began Keemat again.

'The Rani insisted that I bring her to meet the man. He had seen her in the town. Well, the Rani could not understand my refusal. She grew angry. She abused both me and my ancestors. She called my sister a prostitute—for not behaving like one!'

'Did your sister know of all this?' Keemat was finally able to put a question.

'Only afterwards. Naturally I told her and my wife about it.'

134

Keemat Lal gave a low groan. Too many people were coming into his orbit. He wished it had only been the servant, Chotte Lal. But that would have been too simple. The Rani's life had been complex, and her death was likely to lead to further complications. What a way for a high-born woman to make a living! Obviously she had been reduced to desperate measures. Or had it been in her nature to be a procuress?

Dalip Singh . . . Could he have been the mysterious caller whose voice he had heard on the telephone? A wealthy man, who must have kept the Rani in funds, perhaps it was he who had paid the telephone rental for her. Keemat had met Dalip Singh. They had occasionally stood each other drinks in the bar of the Himalaya Hotel. The businessman had come to Mussoorie about two years ago with a rather unsavoury reputation; but during his stay in the hill station, his conduct—in both financial and social matters—had been above reproach.

Keemat Lal stooped again and picked up the meat chopper. He was taking no chances. He would have the blood on the knife analysed, though it would take some time. And if there was human blood on the chopper, he wouldn't hesitate to arrest Bishan Singh.

135

'I'm taking this with me,' he said.

'But, sahib, I do not have another.'

'All the better for you, otherwise I would be forced to take that too. You will get it back in a few days—provided you are innocent!'

Keemat Lal turned to leave. As he did so, his eyes met those of Bishan Singh's sister. She was looking at him with an expression of fierce resentment. Keemat hurriedly took his eyes away from her, and set off down the path.

'Take this to the station,' he told Constable Sant Ram, handing him the chopper. 'It has to go to Lucknow for a blood analysis. It's urgent! I want to know the result as soon as possible. I want to know if the blood on it is animal or human.'

'Very good, sir. And who shall we see now?'

'We are not going to see anyone until after we have had our lunch. Come along.'

VI

Keemat Lal felt a little better after lunch. His wife, sensing his mood, had made a delicious pulao with mutton koftas, and this, served with Keemat's favourite gourd pickle, made the Inspector belch with appreciation. But the rice and mild warmth of the afternoon sun—he had had the meal out on his veranda—made him drowsy, and he felt disinclined

136

to continue with any investigations. He devoutly wished the Rani had got herself murdered elsewhere. And he wished Constable Sant Ram had not finished his own meal so quickly—for here he was, marching in smartly at the Inspector's gate, looking keen and conscientious.

'Well,' reflected Keemat. 'Here's my chance. Solve this murder, find a culprit, and I can be justified in asking for both a promotion and a transfer.' And with one final satisfying belch, he heaved himself out of his comfortable chair and stepped out with Sant Ram.

A half-hour later they were at the bania's shop. Keemat Lal refused a cup of tea, and Sant Ram had to regretfully follow his chief's example.

'For how long have you run this shop?' asked Keemat conversationally.

The bania, an elderly man who had kept himself in fit condition in spite of many years of shopkeeping, said, 'About ten years, Inspector sahib. Before that I was in the Punjab, in my village, working the land. It was after my second marriage that I came here. I have worked hard and saved enough to send my eldest son to college—for today there are no prospects for a young man who has not been to college. And my daughter here, well, in another three years, I hope to have enough for a dowry that will bring her a good husband.'

The bania's wife, whose features still provided evidence of early beauty, smiled maternally at Keemat and urged him to have a cup of tea. The daughter sat on her haunches inside the small low-ceilinged shop. She was only fourteen and her name was Kamla. Her large, dark and very expressive eyes smouldered resentfully. Her feet and hands were rough, but she had long smooth arms, and her breasts were just beginning to form.

The bania mentioned that the girl was going to school. 'But she is a wild one,' he observed, giving Kamla a gloomy look. 'She fights with boys, goes wandering off into the hills, and does not behave as a girl should!'

'Where is her dog?' asked Keemat.

'Oh, it must be somewhere. It is quite independent.'

'The Rani gave it to Kamla?'

'Yes, about three years ago. It was just a puppy. The Rani found it lying in a drain, almost dead from cold and hunger. She fed it and made it strong, and then she gave it to Kamla.'

'She was a kind woman then?'

'But certainly, sahib. Why, has anyone said she was not?'

Keemat made no reply. Instead he said, 'She must have had many friends.'

'Not many . . .'

'And enemies?'

'I do not know.'

'Come, lalaji, you have lived here ten years—almost as long as the Rani. You must have known who her friends and enemies were. We know she was a quarrelsome woman. Who did she quarrel with? Did she fall out with anyone recently?'

'I swear I do not know, sahib. It is true that she had a bad temper. Often she vented it on us. Small things upset her. If children were rude, she would scream at them. She had slapped Kamla more than once. But her anger disappeared rapidly. Ten minutes after abusing us, she would be borrowing our grinding stone.'

Keemat Lal could not suppress his smile. 'You knew her ways well,' he said. 'Others might not have been so forgiving. They might have resented her attitude.'

'That is true,' said the bania, nodding his head wisely. 'There was a misunderstanding once between her and Mrs Kapoor. It was a small matter, but because of it they have not spoken to each other for the last three years. Mr Kapoor tried his best, poor man, but neither woman would make the first move.' The bania, when he got going, could be quite loquacious—he did not need much prompting from Keemat Lal. 'The Rani had introduced Mr Kapoor to another lady, a teacher in the girls' school. Mrs Kapoor did not like it. She accused the Rani of interfering in her private life, and naturally there was a quarrel.'

Keemat nodded encouragingly.

'Well, sahib, that is all. After that, they were always at war with each other. Mrs Kapoor complained that the Rani threw stones on her roof at night, and the Rani accused Mrs Kapoor of bribing her sweeper to leave! Finally, the Rani called in the police. She invited them to a wonderful tea party, and complained of Mrs Kapoor's behaviour. The police called on Mrs Kapoor, who gave them a better tea party—this was before your time, sahib—and later sent the inspector a bottle of whisky. And the complaint was thus disposed of.'

'Well, never mind all that,' said Keemat. 'Who was this teacher you mentioned?'

'A Christian. I forget her name.'

'Was she good-looking?'

'She was dark.'

'I am not asking for her colour, lalaji!'

The bania looked surprised. 'A dark woman cannot be considered good-looking, sahib.' Like many others, he had been brought up to believe that only fair women could be beautiful; this was one reason why he was disappointed with Kamla. She would be at a disadvantage when it came to finding a husband for her.

Keemat was catholic in outlook, at least as far as women were concerned—he saw something attractive in nearly all of them.

'You must be a great judge of beauty, lalaji,' he said dryly.

'The teacher was not beautiful, sahib. She was young and slim and quite clever—but she was dark!'

'Your daughter, too, is dark,' said Keemat.

'I know, it is a great pity.'

Keemat Lal shrugged his shoulders in amusement. He saw no point in getting into an argument with a man too set in his convictions and too old to change them.

'Is the teacher still in Mussoorie?'

'She will not be here now. The school is closed for the winter months, and she spends her holidays somewhere in the plains. But they open in a week or two, and she will be here then—that is, if she continues teaching in this school.'

'And Mrs Kapoor?'

'She lives close by,' said the bania. 'She is here these days. Her husband is away. He is in the army.'

'Right. I will see her later.' He wanted the bania to get to Mrs Kapoor first. Women always revealed more when they were on the defensive. 'But now I want to see Miss Bean, the old English lady.'

The bania chuckled as if at some private joke. 'Just down the hill, Inspector sahib.'

'I am not sure of the way.' Keemat was looking at Kamla, who had not changed her position since his arrival. 'I wonder if your daughter can take me there.'

When the girl made no response, her father turned to her and said, 'Go on, Kamla, take the Inspector sahib to Miss Bean's house. Don't sit there like a dumb creature!'

Kamla rose unwillingly and, without once looking at Keemat Lal, walked ahead of him down the path. She deliberately walked fast, barefooted, so that she could keep some distance between her and the Inspector. But Keemat was determined to have a private word with her. Making a mighty effort, he caught up with the girl. He almost seized her by the wrist, but checked himself in time. He noticed her glass bangles—she wore two green bangles. Surely she ought to have been wearing three? He thought that was the custom but he wasn't too sure of these things.

'Not so fast, Kamla,' he said, 'not so fast. You

are just like my own small daughter, impatient and over-eager.'

Keemat Lal did not have a daughter, only a small boy; but it was a master stroke of deception. Some of the suspicion left the girl's eyes, and she looked at Keemat with more tolerance than before.

'That's better,' he said. 'Walk with me, I want to talk to you. You look like my daughter too, though you are much thinner.'

Kamla looked Keemat Lal up and down, and smiled. Keemat was immediately made conscious of his girth. A slim daughter would have made an unusual contrast! But Kamla was now disposed to be a little friendly, and her confidence was returning. She looked at Keemat as though he were a human being instead of a rakshas!

'Kamla, did you like the Rani very much?'

She nodded her head vigorously, but did not say anything.

'And did the other children like her?'

'They were too small,' she said.

Too small! Too small for what? Too small to have violent likes and dislikes? Keemat looked at the girl with a renewal of interest and with increasing respect. 'Too small to like the Rani?' he asked.

'No. Too small to kill her.'

Keemat Lal almost stumbled in mid-stride. This

girl was always one jump ahead of him. How much did she know? Well, since she was being direct—how refreshing it was to deal with a direct person: a pity it was only children who could afford to be frank—he would also be more to the point in his conversation with her. 'Do you know who killed her, Kamla?'

She gave a deep, weary, adult sigh, and said, 'No, I do not know.'

Keemat Lal also sighed. For a moment he had been certain that the girl would know who had killed the Rani. And perhaps she was covering up now—perhaps she was afraid to reveal what she knew. 'If you know something, please tell me, Kamla. It might help me to catch the murderer. It is dangerous to let a murderer go free. A person who has killed once may kill again.'

'I know,' she said nodding wisely. 'I could not touch lizards. Then one day I killed one. Now it is easy to kill them.' She shook her head again so that her pigtail fell across her shoulder, and said, 'No, I do not know. I did not see anyone.'

'Did you go to see the Rani yesterday evening?'

She hesitated, then said, 'I took her some sugar. She called down to the shop, and papaji sent me up with the sugar.'

'At what time was this, Kamla?'

'I do not know. It was before it became dark.'

'How long before? Try to remember. It is important.'

They had stopped walking, and were now standing together under the whispering deodar trees. The wind soughed gently in the upper branches. They made an odd pair—the Inspector large, circular and self-conscious; the girl small, dark, full of confidence.

'Nearly an hour before it got dark. It must have been about six o'clock.'

'Did you see the butcher?'

'No.'

'Did you see Miss Bean coming down the hill?'

'No, but I saw the missionary sahib. He was in his garden. He waved to me, and said something, but I did not reply. He wants to take me to the church. There are ghosts in churches, are there not?'

'Did anyone come to see the Rani while you were there, or as you were leaving?'

Did she hesitate again—or did she pause only to button up the end of her blouse? It had fallen open to reveal her slim dark waist. 'Nobody came.'

'Did you meet anyone in the road when you were returning to the shop?'

'Only the boys. They were playing cricket.'

'Did you join them?'

'They would not let me play,' she said. 'I watched them for a little while, then I went home.'

They were walking again, and Keemat could see a bright red roof through the cluster of oak trees beneath the path. Very few Mussoorie houses had their roofs painted. The few that did looked like old biscuit tins.

'Were your mother and father in the shop all evening?'

'Oh, yes. That is the time when people come to buy their supplies. They are always in the shop in the evening.'

The trouble was, there were three paths coming from different directions, all meeting near the Rani's house. Her visitor—and killer—could have come by any of them. One path came down the hill past the Simmonses' house, the second passed the bania's shop and rose to the gate of the house, and the third came over the spur of the hill on which the local school was situated.

'Here is the house of the English lady,' said Kamla, pointing down at the little cottage. 'Can I go now?'

'Yes, Kamla, I will see you again. Oh, one minute—did you take your dog with you when you went to see the Rani?'

The girl looked puzzled, a little unsure of herself.
'I don't remember,' she said.

'It doesn't matter,' said Keemat Lal, smiling at
her. 'It isn't important.'

Kamla turned on her heels and went running
uphill with an ease and gazelle-like grace that
Keemat Lal could not help admiring and envying.

VII

'Oh, who is it?' said Miss Bean sharply, as though
she were being constantly pestered by callers, when
in fact she received only one or two visitors a
month. She was in the middle of embroidering a
wallflower pattern on a cushion cover, and almost
thrust the needle into her finger when she heard a
loud knocking at her door.

The knocking was followed by a fit of coughing.
'For heaven's sake, you'll cough your lungs out,'
Miss Bean grumbled at the unknown caller. She
threw down her embroidery in disgust and went to
the door.

For a few seconds after opening the door, she
was unware that someone stood there, so effectively
did Inspector Keemat Lal fill the opening. It was as
though the sun had suddenly been eclipsed. Miss
Bean, a short and by now short-sighted woman,
found herself staring at the bright buttons on Keemat
Lal's tunic.

'Good morning, madam,' said Keemat. He had been brought up to treat his elders with respect, and being confronted by this white-haired but far-from-senile lady of over eighty, he was overcome by a schoolboy awe and bashfulness.

'Good morning, young man,' said Miss Bean, and Keemat's spirits soared at mention of the words 'young man'. Here, at last, was a discerning woman!

'I'm from the police,' he said apologetically.

'Oh, I thought you were the man who comes to check the electric meter. Never mind, come in. I hope I haven't done anything wrong.'

'No, madam, it's only about the murder of the Rani.' Keemat stepped into the room and nearly fell over a small table on which a lot of bric-a-brac was on display. 'You know about it, of course?'

'Oh, yes. I heard about it from the postman. Can you imagine, she may have been lying dead at the very moment I passed her gate yesterday? What an awful thought! Won't you sit down, Constable?'

'Inspector, madam.'

'Oh, it's Inspector, is it?' She looked at him rather doubtfully. 'Well, never mind, do sit down. Don't feel nervous.'

Keemat Lal lowered himself into a well-cushioned cane chair, but realized too late that it was not made for a man of his proportions. He found himself suspended on the arms of the chair, a foot above the cushions. To be on the safe side, and to avoid looking ridiculous a second time, he perched himself uncomfortably on a small stool. Miss Bean returned to her chair by the window and took up her embroidery. Her demeanor made Keemat feel like an over-grown schoolboy.

Keemat's eyes were slowly growing accustomed to the darkness of the room. It was crowded with furniture, knick-knacks, framed photographs of men and women dressed in Victorian clothes—the men sporting untidy drooping moustaches—books by Ella Wheeler Wilcox and Maude Diver, and numerous jam and pickle bottles converted into flower-vases. On the walls were a number of watercolours, mainly of sunsets and Damascus roses, probably painted by Miss Bean herself. The vases were filled with wild primroses and saxifrage.

'Lovely weather, isn't it?' remarked Miss Bean, finding the Inspector's silence a little irksome. 'If I were ten years younger, I'd be out hiking. But time creeps up on one very swiftly, you know. Still, as long as I have my garden, I've nothing to complain about.'

'You have been in Mussoorie a long time, haven't you, madam?'

'Sixty years. My father brought me here when I was just a chit of a girl. He retired from the army— Royal Artillery, wounded in World War I—and then bought this cottage. I buried him in Mussoorie and I buried my brother and sister here too. That was a long time ago. I've lived alone these last twenty years.'

'Why did you not go to England after Independence?'

'I was too old to think of starting my life all over again. In England, they don't let you work once you're over fifty-five. After that, it's the pensioners' home, cooped up with a lot of other old people. I know, I have friends there. Well, I don't have any money now, but I have my own roof over my head, and I have my garden and I have the sun for nine months in the year . . .'

'Do you live all alone?' asked Keemat. 'Don't you keep a servant?'

'I can't afford one. Had dozens once. But I manage quite well on my own.'

'You had tea with Mr and Mrs Simmons yesterday,' said Keemat, coming back to business without any warning. 'And you left their place at about six o'clock?'

'Pardon? Oh, Joan and John! Yes, it was just before six when I left.'

'When you passed the Rani's gate, did you look in?'

'She was no more a rani than you or I! And I have never looked in at her gate, Inspector.'

'I am sorry. I did not mean to be rude.'

'Oh, I don't think you are being rude. It's just that Nita and I were not on speaking terms.'

'Oh, I see.'

'So I usually looked the other way when I passed her house.'

'You could not have seen anyone who was in her compound at the time?'

'I would probably have noticed someone coming or going. But there was no one, just a bunch of children playing cricket, or whatever that game with sticks is called—guli danda—very dangerous . . . I was struck once by a flying splinter! You ought to do something to stop it.'

'Yes, madam, certainly. You were saying . . . er, what were you saying?'

'That I was not on good terms with your Rani.' Miss Bean stiffened a back that was already very straight. 'I don't think anyone was on good terms with her. But it's not for me to speak ill of someone who can no longer defend herself—though she attacked enough people in her lifetime. Doubtless you'll pick up some juicy titbits in the course of your enquiry.'

'I have heard a little,' said Keemat, 'but it is not much to go on.'

Miss Bean's eyebrows shot up. They were magnificent eyebrows, and many years of practice had given them considerable mobility. 'Mussoorie must be more discreet than I had imagined,' she said. 'Hasn't Mrs Kapoor told you anything?'

'I have not seen her yet. I have been very busy— there are so many people to see—and I have to *walk* from place to place. In the plains, I had a jeep at my disposal.'

'Poor man, your feet must be quite sore.'

Keemat Lal was about to enlarge on their soreness, but checked himself in time. 'Did you have any personal enmity for the Rani?' he asked.

'I hadn't spoken to her for almost six years.'

'Oh, why was that?'

'She cheated me once. I was hard up at the time, and had to sell a lot of my good furniture and china. She said she had a buyer for me, and took over a few thousand rupees' worth of stuff, giving me a small advance. I never saw the rest of the money. Later she flatly denied that she owed me anything.'

'That was a very mean thing to do,' said Keemat sympathetically.

'Well, it was my fault, I suppose, for having

trusted her. I had been warned. But she had been quite good to me when she first came here. I know what you're thinking, Sergeant—or did you say Inspector? I didn't kill Nita. I would like to have killed her, I'll admit that—six years ago! I don't think I care enough now. Do you know how old I am?'

'Over eighty, I am told, but you look much younger. And quite strong!'

Miss Bean chortled with pleasure. 'I'm strong enough to look after my garden, and cook my breakfast and dinner. It's funny, I could never cook as a girl. But adversity teaches one a lot of things, including humility. That was your so-called Rani's trouble—she had no humility. We had both seen better days, but she refused to believe they were over for her.'

Keemat Lal rose to leave. 'Please don't get up,' he said. 'I know the way.' At the door, he stooped and picked up a small axe that was resting against the wall. 'What do you use an axe for?' he asked.

Miss Bean's eyebrows curved upwards. 'Now what would anyone be using an axe for, Inspector? For chopping wood, of course!'

'You mean you chop wood too?'

'Well, I don't intend to freeze to death. Yes, I know it's against the law to cut trees, but these are just fallen branches that I split up. It's quite easy once you have learnt the knack of it.'

Keemat took a closer look at Miss Bean, and noticed that she possessed strong wrists and fairly thick arms, on which only a few varicose veins showed.

'If I'm as healthy at eighty as you are,' he said wryly, 'I'll be a lucky man.'

'If you get to be eighty,' said Miss Bean with a gentle smile, and Keemat noticed that she glanced meaningfully at his midriff. He made a hurried departure.

He was some thirty feet up the slope and was just pausing to recover his breath, when he heard Miss Bean hailing him from below. 'You've left your cap behind,' she called. And so he had. Down again to the cottage, and up once more to the top of the path, his trousers full of thorns and prickly leaves. 'Would you like a cup of tea, Inspector?' Keemat had just enough breath left to reply, 'No thank you, Miss Bean. Some other time.' And who was it had told him the old lady couldn't hurt a fly?

VIII

As Inspector Keemat Lal toiled homewards, the sun sank below the western foothills. It left the sky a deep bloody red, like an exposed wound. But

Keemat, though at times an appreciative observer of the splendours of nature, was in no mood for sunsets. He was feeling embittered at the undignified mien he presented in this case. Just fancy, an inspector of police having to trudge from house to house like an itinerant pedlar! From a jeep he would have commanded authority and respect, he would have been able to conceal the fact that he was not very fit, and, most important, he would have been able to move about much quicker. It was twenty-four hours since the murder of the Rani, and he had not yet been able to question two very important people—Dalip Singh and Mrs Kapoor, both of whom had been closely connected with the dead woman.

He had a few small mercies to be thankful for. The overall picture was becoming a little clearer. He now had some ideas about the character of the dead woman. She had been a rather selfish and at times ruthless individual; a person who had lost money and position but not the desire for power and authority; a person of few principles who did not hesitate to aid the corruption of young women if it paid her dividends. A desperate woman of few talents, none of which could bring her a living. A brow-beater and a bully—she would have done well in the police force, reflected Keemat. Yet she

was capable at times of sudden acts of kindness—
a kindness that was as rare and unpredictable as
sunshine on a monsoon day. Beneath all the bluster
and connivance, perhaps there had been a
vulnerability, a core of sensitivity.

She was a woman to scorn, avoid and pity. A
woman to hate and, finally, to kill. And of the
people Keemat had seen so far, how many were
capable of murder?

The Simmonses' connection with the Rani seemed
very remote. They had not known her for long, and
apparently they had not been involved in any of her
schemes, even as victims. But why had Mr Simmons
stated that he had seen the butcher at the Rani's
gate a little before six o'clock? The butcher had
insisted that it had been nearer five, though of
course that still made it possible for him to have
committed the murder. And he admitted to a quarrel.
But neither Miss Bean nor Kamla had seen the
butcher when they were near the house at six.
Simmons would have to be questioned again.

Then there was Chotte Lal, the Rani's unpaid
servant. She had done him a favour once, got him
a job in the bank—one of her rare acts of kindness.
How much did he know of the Rani's innermost
secrets? How far did she trust him? The man
behaved like an ignoramus, became tongue-tied

when questioned. Surely there was more to be got out of him . . .

And the butcher. If the Rani had plotted the seduction of his sister, he might well have struck her down with his chopper in a fit of rage. But Keemat had nothing against him yet—unless, of course, the meat chopper had more than pigs' blood on it.

The bania and his wife? They lived close enough to the Rani's house. One of them could have slipped out of the shop for a few minutes without being noticed. But they had no apparent motive and, to Keemat, they seemed unlikely murderers. The bania had a tolerant easy-going nature; such men seldom resorted to sudden violence.

Of course the girl Kamla knew something, he was certain of that. And she was keeping her knowledge to herself. He would have to make another attempt to gain her confidence.

And the old lady? Well, he wouldn't put it past her. She must have a sadistic streak in her, to let him get to the top of the steep path a second time before offering him a cup of tea! That rankled a little . . . Or perhaps she didn't have any tea, and was putting a brave face on it. In which case, thought Keemat, poor old thing . . .

He had reached the Mall, and the bar of the

Himalaya Hotel was open. Keemat Lal stepped in for a refresher. He was badly in need of one.

IX

The following morning, after informing Mr Dalip Singh on the telephone that he would be calling on him, Keemat Lal set out for what he fully expected would be another gruelling day spent clambering like an overweight goat along precipitous mountain paths. He had changed his shoes for sandals. It was a little warmer than the previous day, and the primroses on the hillsides and supporting walls had burst into bright little pink and blue flowers. Wild saxifrage thrust their pale pink stems through rocks and briefly opened their petals to the mild sunshine.

Dalip Singh's large house was kept in fairly good condition. Several palm trees, planted in Victorian times, presented an odd contrast to the magnificent deodars on the slopes above the house.

Dalip Singh was a square heavy man, but he lacked both the height and girth of Keemat Lal. He was dressed immaculately in western clothes, and smoked an expensive cigar. His confidence could be sensed by others and he almost smelt of wealth. This made Keemat—who was neither confident nor wealthy—more than usually aggressive. Even the offer of a whisky and soda did not mollify him, but he accepted the drink.

Keemat avoided Dalip Singh's eyes and fixed his gaze on the deerskin that adorned the sitting room wall. 'I think you telephoned the Rani the day after she was killed.' He had decided to get straight to the matter at hand.

Unperturbed, Dalip Singh said, 'Yes, I phoned her. Someone picked up the receiver at the other end, but as nothing was said, I hung up. Could it have been you, Inspector?'

'Yes,' said Keemat, realizing that he was dealing with a shrewd and intelligent man. 'It was the morning after we found the body. You hadn't been to see her the previous evening, had you?'

'No . . . Actually, I was supposed to see her, but I wasn't feeling too well. The reason I rang up was to tell her why I couldn't come.'

'What did you want to see her about?'

'Oh, just a personal matter.'

'The Rani was murdered, Mr Singh. All personal matters now become police matters. They need not of course become public matters.'

'Even if they have no bearing on her death?'

'And who is to be the judge of that? We don't know what bears on her death, and what doesn't— at least I don't! Therefore everything bears on her death.'

Dalip Singh emptied his glass. Keemat's was

already empty, but his host did not offer to refill it.

'It was about a loan I had given her,' said Dalip Singh. 'We had been friends for a long time. Recently I made her a small loan.'

'Interest?'

'None at all.'

'When you phoned, did you intend asking her to return the money?'

Dalip Singh smiled indulgently, as if he found all these questions very silly but was willing to humour the Inspector.

'It was only a small amount,' he said. 'Two thousand rupees. I am fairly well off, Inspector, and can afford to pay my taxes. Nita was at liberty to return the amount whenever she liked. We were good friends.'

Keemat did not like Dalip Singh's patronizing smile. 'Was it a loan?' he asked. 'Or a payment on account?'

Dalip Singh looked puzzled. 'I don't understand. Payment for what?'

'I'm asking you.'

'I don't follow, Inspector.' Dalip Singh shook his head in apparent bewilderment. 'I did not owe her any money, if that's what you are implying. Nor had she sold me anything.'

'Had she done you any favours?' pressed Keemat Lal.

'Oh, she had been a good friend to me. She was very kind to my wife and daughter.'

'Your family is here?'

'No, they are in Delhi. They will come up next week when the schools reopen.'

'And in the meantime you are living alone?'

'Yes.'

'Don't you find it lonely?'

'Sometimes. But I'm negotiating some business deals in the area, and have had to stay up here most of the winter for that.'

'And how do you amuse yourself?'

Dalip Singh gestured in the direction of the whisky bottle.

'You don't feel the need for a woman?' persisted Keemat, determined to trap the businessman into making an indiscreet remark.

'Well, who wouldn't? I am looking forward to the arrival of my wife.'

'A loyal husband,' said Keemat with approval. 'They are very rare nowadays.'

'Well, I won't say I haven't indulged in a few indiscretions now and then. Haven't you, Inspector?'

Keemat was at a loss for a reply. Finally he asked, 'But do you *buy* your indiscretions, Mr Singh?'

'What exactly do you mean?' The businessman

was beginning to look angry—which was just what Keemat wanted.

'There is a rumour going about that the Rani supplied you with women. Rather young women, I understand.'

Dalip Singh seemed on the verge of losing his temper, then suddenly he slapped his thighs and burst into laughter. Was his hilarity a little forced or was it genuine? Keemat found it difficult to tell.

'If it weren't for rumours,' said Dalip Singh, 'this town would indeed be a dull place. I can assure you, Inspector, that it is only a rumour without any substance. Certainly I have known many women, but they have always been perfectly respectable friendships!'

Keemat did not, at this juncture, wish to mention the butcher's sister. 'I'll take your word for it,' he said, and got up to leave.

When they were at the gate, he asked, 'Do you have any idea why anyone should want to kill the Rani?'

'None at all,' said Dalip Singh. 'Are you sure nothing was missing from the house? Perhaps she surprised a thief, and he killed her in a panic. That has often happened.'

'True. But as far as we know, nothing was missing. Unfortunately, we do not know if she had anything of real value. Yes, it could have been a thief, Mr Singh, but it must have been a thief who was known to her. Otherwise he could hardly have entered the house when there were so many people about. The Rani was killed before seven. It may have been a stranger—but I'm willing to bet you a bottle of whisky that it was someone she knew quite well!'

X

Mrs Kapoor was a handsome woman. She must have been about thirty, and she combined a certain maturity with good looks. She had a firm and well-proportioned figure. A boy of five or six, her only child, was kicking a ball about the garden when Keemat Lal arrived. The boy ran indoors to call his mother, while Keemat sank into one of the two cane chairs that stood on a small lawn. He had barely made himself comfortable when Mrs Kapoor appeared. He was grateful to her for motioning to him to remain seated.

Basking in the warm sunshine, his back well-cushioned, his eyes comforted by Mrs Kapoor's soothing outline, Keemat concluded that at least this interview would not be unpleasant.

'Will you have some tea?' asked the lady.

Keemat was about to reply in the negative, as

was his habit by now. But then he thought, why not? Surely he could make an exception occasionally. And Mrs Kapoor was certainly exceptional. 'If it isn't any trouble,' he said gallantly.

'No trouble at all.' And beckoning to her small son, she said, 'Romesh, tell Nandu to bring some tea out here—and some hot cheese pakoras!' Mrs Kapoor rose even higher in Keemat Lal's estimation. Pakoras—especially if they were hot and made of cheese—were his favourite snack.

Keemat made some admiring remarks about the garden and little Romesh's looks, and Mrs Kapoor in turn said complimentary things about the local police force. It was the first time Keemat had heard someone praising the police, and Mrs Kapoor's words acted as balm to both his soul and conscience. Nor did it take long for tea to arrive.

'Where is your husband nowadays?' asked Keemat, helping himself to the largest pakora.

'Somewhere in Assam. He is with the border force. But he hopes to obtain some leave this summer, and then he will come up to Mussoorie.'

'Excellent,' said Keemat heartily, almost hoping that his investigations might now drag on till the summer months. 'How do you pass your time here?'

'I give tuitions once the schools open. I shall

probably be busy with two or three pupils from next week.'

'And what do you teach them?'

'Hygiene and physiology.'

'Physiology is most interesting,' said Keemat enthusiastically.

'Hygiene is too.'

'Oh, hygiene too, certainly!' He helped himself to a third pakora, spilt a little tea on his uniform, and then decided to get down to business. 'Your neighbour, the late Rani, did you know her very well?'

'Yes, quite well. We had been neighbours for several years. How terrible for her to have been killed like that! I suppose you are busy trying to find out who did it.'

'Yes, madam. Frankly, I am finding it very difficult. Do you have any ideas on the subject?'

'I, Inspector? I haven't really thought much about it. You don't think it was a thief?'

'We don't know if anything was missing.'

'Did you examine her jewellery box?'

'Naturally. We found a few semi-precious stones, and a gold signet ring with her husband's initials.'

'I think she owned a valuable diamond ring. I saw her wearing it once or twice. It should have been worth a fair amount. But she may have sold or pawned it.'

Keemat Lal made a mental note of this information. He had not found a diamond ring amongst the Rani's effects. That meant he would have to visit the jewellers' shops in the bazaar to see if any of them had it now. 'Do you know if the Rani had any enemies?' he asked.

'She was not very popular,' said Mrs Kapoor distantly. 'I suppose its possible for someone to have hated her. She could be very mean—and sometimes even abusive! I kept my son out of her way—she had the evil eye.'

'And you, madam, were you on good terms with her?'

Mrs Kapoor hesitated, then gave a slight shrug and said, 'We did not get on very well. There had been some differences of opinion, and the Rani was quite insulting.'

Keemat felt relieved that Mrs Kapoor was not trying to conceal too much. 'Had your husband met her?' he asked.

'Yes, two or three years ago.' She was obviously unwilling to elucidate any further. But as an afterthought, she added, 'She wasn't young enough to attract him in any way, if that's what you are thinking.'

'Far from it,' said Keemat hastily, aware that he was now treading on delicate ground. 'I can't imagine your husband bothering to look at anyone else.'

'You're very flattering, Inspector.'

If Keemat could have blushed, he would have done so. The tips of his ears felt very hot, which was the nearest he ever came to blushing. But his next question ruined the goodwill that he had been building up. 'Do you know Mr Dalip Singh?' he asked innocently.

'You mean the property dealer?' Mrs Kapoor's expression was no longer friendly and tolerant. 'I don't know him very well.'

'But you have met him?'

'Yes, once or twice. I did not like him.'

'I did not think you would, madam. Was it the Rani who introduced you to him?'

'Yes, at a party a year or so ago. Mr Singh was very forward. He seemed to be of the opinion that women could not fail to succumb to his charm. An ugly great hulk of a man . . .' Mrs Kapoor checked herself when she noticed that Keemat was looking a trifle embarrassed, and, realizing that he was as large as Dalip Singh and even more rotund, she paused a moment before continuing. 'He has no manners, only appetites. Appetites for food, drink and women. But he'll overstep himself one of these days,' she concluded mysteriously.

Keemat cleared his throat before asking his next question. 'Do you know if he was . . . er . . . very close . . . intimate . . . with the Rani?'

'I suppose he must have been,' said Mrs Kapoor without any hesitation. 'He wouldn't have bothered to come and see her so regularly otherwise.'

'Probably not. Unless she was acting as an intermediary between him and some other woman.'

'I don't know about that.' Mrs Kapoor seemed thoughtful, and Keemat sensed a core of hardness, of calculation, beneath her surface charm. 'It is possible, of course. There was a teacher in the girls'school—I forget her name—she was always trying to hook a wealthy man.'

Keemat proved to be a heartless sort of admirer. 'Your husband met this teacher once, didn't he? I think it was the Rani who introduced them.'

Mrs Kapoor was momentarily confused. Then, suddenly angry, she said, 'The Rani had no business doing that. She hardly knew my husband. I'm sure it was just to spite me!'

Keemat nodded sympathetically, swiftly put away the last cheese pakora, and rose unwillingly from his chair. He was afraid he had spoilt his chance of making himself popular with Mrs Kapoor. Well, a policeman never has a chance with beautiful women, he reflected. Either he is resented, or made use of

. . . And Mrs Kapoor, it seemed, was going to be the resentful type.

Compared to the warmth of his reception, Keemat's departure from the premises was a chilly affair.

XI

When he was walking back to town, Keemat saw Kamla, the bania's daughter, perched on a rock high up on the hillside. She had washed her hair, and it lay open across her shoulders, drying in the sun. She saw Keemat Lal and smiled down at him, secure in the knowledge that he could not follow her up the steep slope. Keemat beckoned to her to come down, but she chose that moment to look away. When he called out, she seemed not to hear him.

'Damn,' said Keemat Lal. He had never before been thwarted from questioning a suspect merely because he was unable to climb a precipitous hill. It was not that he considered the girl a suspect— only that he was certain she knew something that could be of vital importance. And apparently she had no intention of revealing her secret.

Now the butcher's sister, she was an altogether different proposition. She was an attractive wench, and she had plenty of motive. Even if her brother had not killed the Rani, it was quite possible that she had done so. Perhaps the girl's family knew of it, and perhaps they didn't. Even if the guilty one was known to the entire butcher fraternity in Mussoorie, these people were loyal to one another and would not readily disclose their knowledge to the police.

Keemat reflected that this attitude was a relic of colonial times when the police had been looked upon as a willing instrument of foreign oppression. Now, though it was over twenty-five years since Independence, the police were still unpopular. They had not, of course, always acted with fairness or impartiality. The many cases of corruption and excesses that had come to light had all but convinced the ordinary man that it was best to keep at a safe distance from the long—and sometimes crooked—arm of the law. Thus, even a conscientious and fundamentally decent individual like Keemat Lal found the going difficult in any sort of investigation.

And here, as though she had sprung naturally from his thoughts, was the butcher's sister. She was walking down the road and would have to pass Keemat. He could not help admiring her splendid physique and the dignity of her walk.

To Keemat's intense surprise, the butcher's sister smiled at him. He stammered a greeting as he passed, and then gaped in astonishment at her receding figure. It had been his impression that she was a young woman too modest to smile at a complete stranger, and this friendliness did not fit in with the hostility she had shown him the previous day.

He wondered if she was trying to be clever. Or did she think his suspicions, whatever they were, could be allayed by a more friendly approach? Perhaps she was not as innocent as the butcher had affirmed. And perhaps, thought Keemat wryly, she had been more willing to comply with the Rani's wishes than her brother would have him believe.

He was on his way to the bazaar when he met Mr and Mrs Simmons. The missionary's wife was pushing a pram, which made Keemat realize for the first time that the couple were parents. The baby was about four months old, and looked like most babies of that age—pink, soft and dribbling at the mouth. Keemat made some appropriately complimentary remarks about the child, feasted his eyes on Joan Simmon's cream-smooth neck and shoulders, and reluctantly gave his attention to Mr Simmons.

'Do you mind clearing up one point for me?' he asked. 'You said you had seen the butcher at the

Rani's house at six o'clock on the evening she was killed.'

'Oh, did I?' said Simmons, looking slightly bewildered.

'I noted it down,' said Keemat patiently. 'You may have to testify to that in court.'

Simmons looked unhappy. His eyelids fluttered behind his spectacles. 'Obviously I must have said so. I did not think it was very important. Yes, of course, I do remember seeing the butcher at the Rani's house. They were having an argument!'

'So you told me before. But you are sure it was at six o'clock?'

'It was about six o'clock, Inspector. I wouldn't say it was exactly six. What do a few minutes matter in a place like Mussoorie?'

'They don't matter normally. But we are now dealing with a murder. The butcher says it was about five o'clock when he was with the Rani.'

'Oh, does he? Well, perhaps he was. Perhaps I'm mistaken. There's only a difference of an hour.'

'An hour can make all the difference in the world,' said Keemat in an injured tone. 'In your own country, such carelessness about the time would not be forgiven. Because we in India are not so— how shall I put it?—committed to being on time in everything, it doesn't mean we cannot try to sort things out.'

'Of course you are right, Inspector. But I thought it was six o'clock because that's the time Miss Bean left us.'

'Miss Bean says she didn't see the butcher.'

'Perhaps not. They might have missed each other by a few minutes.'

'Isn't it possible, Mr Simmons, that you saw the butcher at five, or thereabouts, when Miss Bean was coming, not going?'

Simmons looked startled, then confused. 'It might have been earlier, I suppose,' he said unhappily. 'But I could have sworn it was nearer six.'

'You may well have to swear one thing or the other,' said Keemat slyly.

Mrs Simmons came to her husband's rescue. Bestowing on Keemat a smile that would have melted the heart of the most hardened magistrate, she said, 'We're so sorry to have caused so much confusion, Mr Lal. John is a little absent-minded at times. It might have been five and it might have been six. But we do hope it wasn't the butcher who killed the Rani. He seems such a decent sort of person—and he has a family! Most murderers are single persons, don't you agree?'

Keemat did not agree, but it was his turn to be apologetic. 'Oh, there's no confusion caused, madam. That is, no confusion that wasn't already there.

You see, the Rani could have been killed at five or six or even seven, we can't fix the exact time. So it may have been the butcher or the bania or Miss Bean or even your husband!' And with a friendly but slightly sinister wave of his hand, Keemat sauntered down the bazaar road.

XII

The Landour bazaar was nearly a mile long. Many of the shops were over a hundred years old, and had known three generations of owners. The narrow cobbled road which ran between the crooked two-storeyed buildings looked almost Dickensian. Sudden gaps in the buildings revealed glimpses of the hills, but the sun had little chance of reaching the pavement except at noon. When snow melted, the road was slippery and dangerous, and then even the sure-footed mountain mules came down on their shoulders or haunches.

Fortunately for Keemat, there were no mules to hinder his progress when he went to visit the three jewellers' shops in the bazaar. Each of the shopkeepers offered Keemat a chair and a cup of tea. Being tired and thirsty, he drank cups of hot sweet tea at each shop. He was beginning to get into the Mussoorie way of doing things—the Mussoorie way of doing nothing.

The shopkeepers were affable and answered all his questions. The Rani had indeed sold or pawned various small items of jewellery, and some of these items were still in their keeping; but none had seen or handled a diamond ring.

Keemat Lal was puzzled. Could Mrs Kapoor have invented the ring? And what could be her reason for doing so? If a ring had in fact existed, then its disappearance was certainly very odd—and of some definite significance . . .

He did not find it difficult to get into a friendly conversation with Pooran Prakash, one of the shopkeepers.

'Do you know Mrs Kapoor, a neighbour of the Rani's?'

'Oh, yes, she is a good customer. One of the few who does not buy things on credit.'

Pooran Prakash drew on the pipe of the beautifully ornamented hookah he was smoking, and waited for Keemat's next question with a quizzical look.

'She was not on good terms with the Rani, was she?'

'Ah!'

'What do you mean, "ah"?'

'I mean I am in agreement with you. The ladies did not like each other. But women seldom get on well with their own kind. They can't help it, of course.'

'You are quite a philosopher. You are right, of course, and I know all about the Rani and Mrs Kapoor hurling stones and abuse at each other. But tell me, did they really hate each other? Petty jealousy isn't sufficient . . .'

Keemat broke off, but Pooran Prakash took his mouth away from his pipe and said, 'For murder? Probably not, Inspector sahib. But the Rani had the habit of going a little too far in some of her feuds. She was from some small principality of little significance, but she clung to her feudal ways and felt that her title gave her special privileges . . . And she had a slanderous tongue. She saw to it that all Mussoorie knew that Mrs Kapoor's son had been born before, or very soon after, her wedding. Probably untrue—not that we cared to know, but . . . Well, you can understand how Mrs Kapoor must have felt. It is quite possible that they hated each other. And murder was possible, too. But it is not as simple as that, Inspector sahib, because the Rani slandered a good many other people as well, and there are few who are sorry to hear that she is dead. Why, she had even put the police on to me once, out of pure spite.'

'Why, were you smuggling gold bars into the country?'

'No, no, Inspector sahib. Merely a matter of putting a little opium in my pipe. But we all have our little weaknesses, don't we?' And he gave Keemat Lal an enigmatic smile.

XIII

Disappointed, Keemat began walking back to his office. On his way, he stepped into a small restaurant and asked to use the telephone. He liked Dalip Singh only for one reason: the man had a telephone in his house and could be reached without a long climb.

He asked for the businessman's number, and soon heard his confident aggressive voice.

'This is Inspector Keemat Lal.'

'Good afternoon, Inspector. What can I do for you?'

'It's just a minor point,' said Keemat. 'As you were a friend of the Rani's, I thought you might know if she had ever possessed a diamond ring.'

There was a slight pause at the other end. Was the man trying to remember or was he thinking up a story? 'I think she had a diamond ring.' Dalip Singh sounded uncertain. 'I never saw her personal things, and I certainly never saw her wearing a diamond ring. But she may have mentioned that she had one. Yes, I seem to remember her mentioning a ring.'

'But you never saw her wearing it?'

'I'm not sure, Inspector. I don't remember. Is there anything else you want to know?'

'That's all,' said Keemat thoughtfully, putting down the phone.

He returned to the police station, attended to some routine matters, asked if the report on the butcher's chopper had arrived—it hadn't—and then learnt that the Rani's cremation was to take place within the hour.

'You had better attend it,' he told Constable Sant Ram.

'Very good, sir. Shall I wear my uniform?'

'Of course. The public must know that the police is always sympathetic towards the victims— even if we can't catch their murderers!'

Keemat had reached the front steps when he was struck by a notion that both attracted and repelled him. He would attend the cremation ceremony himself. It would give him a chance to see who felt impelled to be present during the rites. He was repelled, not by the idea of attending a cremation—which was normal enough—but by the prospect of the very long walk to the cremation grounds, which lay beside a stream at the bottom of a steep ravine. It was almost a thousand feet below Mussoorie, and he would have to climb all the way up afterwards—that is, if he survived the descent!

But his natural curiosity overcame his habitual lethargy. After telling Sant Ram to go home, he set out by himself for the cremation ground.

The bier, drapped in saffron cloth, was carried down the hill on the shoulders of Chotte Lal, the Rani's erstwhile servant, and three friends of his. Behind them came the bania, with a grave expression; one or two other shopkeepers; Dalip Singh, wearing a long black coat buttoned up to the neck; and a small, dark, dapper-looking man whom Keemat had not seen before.

Keemat himself brought up the rear. There were no women present. There were no tears. A band of monkeys gibbered at the procession from the branches of the oak trees.

The wood was damp, and it took some time to light the pyre. But when the fire got going, the oak logs burnt well, sending long plumes of smoke into the deodars.

Finally, when the body had disappeared into a mass of ashes, the small group began the tedious ascent back to town. The stranger walked ahead of the others, and Keemat had to make a great effort to catch up with him.

'I am Inspector Keemat Lal,' he said by way of introduction.

'How do you do?' The stranger was polite but non-committal. He spoke good English.

'We haven't met before, have we?' asked Keemat.

'No, I arrived in Mussoorie only this morning.'

'Oh, I see. You were a friend of the Rani's?'

'Her brother. You telegraphed me yesterday, notifying me of her death.'

'Oh yes, of course.' Keemat remembered having found some addresses amongst the Rani's papers and passing them on to a subordinate for 'appropriate action'. 'We did not think anyone would come. But of course, being her brother it is only natural . . .' He was getting out of breath trying to keep up with the little man. 'You are, then, a rajpramukh or something?'

'Just something,' said the little man with a wry smile. 'My title is no longer an advantage. And as you probably know, we did not really rule a state. Some called it a state but it was only a large zamindari. There is very little left of it now, and it brings in a paltry income. I am now an insurance agent, Inspector. Are you, by the way, insured?'

'No, but I have a provident fund. Tell me, was your sister's life insured?'

'Not by me. I had not seen her for over ten years.'

'Ten years! But you were her brother.'

'She did not get on very well with the rest of the family. She preferred to cut herself off from us. It is a pity because we could have helped her. But she would have nothing to do with us, even in her loneliness. She was a stubborn woman. You see, she had married against our wishes and advice. And when her husband left her, she was too proud to admit that we had been right or even to face us. In fact, after her husband deserted her, she was unreasonable enough to resent us even more!'

'Yes, she must have been a bitter lonely woman,' said Keemat. 'Still, it was good of you to come up.'

'It is right that someone from the family should be here. And I want to see her lawyer, if she had one. It concerns her share in the family property.' He did not elucidate and Keemat did not press him, for his attention had been drawn to Chotte Lal. He noticed for the first time that Chotte had been drinking—and now was stumbling along in the rear, casting dark glaces at everyone, and singing a rather suggestive song. It seemed to annoy Dalip Singh, who lengthened his stride and soon left the others behind. The bania finally fell back to assist Chotte up the remaining portion of the climb.

XIV

Keemat was alone in the bar of the Himalaya Hotel, brooding over a glass of brandy. It was eight

181

o'clock. At home, his dinner would be ready, his small son asleep, and his wife waiting for him to return. It was only after he had eaten that she had her own meal. But there was time for a second brandy, and ordering one, he set himself to the task of drawing up a mental list of 'suspects'—persons involved in the life and affairs of the Rani who might have had the motive, opportunity and desire to get rid of her.

Most of them had one motive in common—a vigorous dislike, even hatred, for the woman—but this in itself was probably insufficient a reason for killing her. The days of witch-hunting were over. Or were they? In Keemat's experience, most murders were committed for some material gain, especially in cities. Those that resulted from a feud, jealousy or sudden unreasoning anger were usually confined to rural areas, where people often acted on the spur of the moment, oblivious of the consequences.

At the same time, the Rani's murder did not appear to be a premeditated affair. Keemat had the impression that it was quite spontaneous. It could have been the result of a quarrel, a sudden flaring of tempers; or it may have been committed by a comparative stranger, a thief who knew something of her ways. A valuable diamond ring would certainly attract a thief, provided he knew of its approximate whereabouts. Had he been surprised by the Rani, he might well have used the axe to silence her. But would a thief break into a house—or walk into an open house—at six o'clock in the evening while it was still light? Surely he would wait until it grew darker?

Keemat made a mental list of the people 'involved', placing them in order of importance:

1. Dalip Singh, businessman, property dealer, a friend of the Rani's for a number of years. He had probably lent her money from time to time. If it was true that she was acting as a procuress for him, it was possible that he had paid her for her help. Opportunity: he could have visited her briefly between four and seven, without being seen. Motive: the Rani, presumably knowing about his private life, might have been blackmailing him.

2. Bishan Singh, the butcher. Opportunity: he had been seen quarrelling with the Rani between five and six on the evening of the murder. Motive: on his own admission, the quarrel had been because the Rani had been trying to bully him into sending his sister to Dalip Singh. She may have had some hold over the butcher which could account for her trying to force him, and this would give him additional motivation. He also had an obvious weapon—his chopper.

3. Mrs Kapoor. She had known the Rani for several years, but had become antagonistic towards her. Opportunity: well, she lived near enough. Motive: the Rani had apparently tried to interest Mrs Kapoor's husband in another woman, and had spread slanderous rumours about Mrs Kapoor's private life. Hardly an adequate motive, but it was possible that Mrs Kapoor was keeping something back, perhaps something fairly substantial. But would she have used an axe? An axe was not an educated woman's weapon—poison would have been more in her line.

4. The butcher's sister. The same motive as her brother. Possibly they could have acted in concert. Having been brought up in the precincts of a slaughter-house, she would not have been squeamish about using an axe or chopper.

5. Chotte Lal, the part-time servant. He had discovered the body and had come straight to the police. Either he was a shrewd and calculating villian, or he was the simpleton that Keemat believed him to be. The Rani had found work for him once, and he had been sufficiently grateful to do odd jobs for her gratis. There was no likely motive—unless he had taken the ring. He had been seen in the bazaar between five and seven, but it would not have taken him more than twenty minutes to reach

the Rani's house and return. And why was he drunk at the funeral?

6. The Simmonses. Neighbours of the Rani, but apparently not very well known to her. No likely motive—but you could never tell with missionaries!

7. The bania and his wife. They had known the Rani for many years, though never intimately. And having kept their distance, they had never quarrelled seriously. Tha bania knew the Rani's nature, and understood the reasons for her unpopularity. He seemed a rational man, though conservative in outlook. Opportunity existed, but no discernible motive.

8. Miss Bean. Eighty-four, but still strong enough to wield an axe. She made no bones about disliking the Rani, who had once—allegedly—cheated her. She had been near the Rani's house at a convenient time. But if she had wanted to kill the Rani, why had she not made the attempt years ago when her resentment was still strong? Or had it grown stronger?

9. Kamla, the bania's daughter. She was concealing something from Keemat. He was almost certain that she knew the identity of the murderer. But she was afraid—for herself or for someone else?

Keemat sighed wearily and emptied his glass. Suddenly realizing that he was terribly hungry, he ceased his ruminations and started for home.

After a dinner of curried mutton with spinach and spring onions, and his favourite masur dal, he settled down in his warm bed for a good night's sleep. He intended to sleep until eight in the morning; but it was not yet six when he was rudely awakened by someone hammering on the front door.

'Shall I see who it is?' said Mrs Keemat Lal, sitting up in bed and reaching for the light switch.

'Better not,' said Keemat, emerging from the bedclothes like an unhappy walrus. He fumbled under the mattress for his revolver. The hammering on the front door continued, accompanied by shouting.

When Keemat Lal opened the door, he found himself confronted by Constable Sant Ram; and Sant Ram found himself looking down the barrel of Keemat's revolver.

'Oh, it's you!' said Keemat lowering his gun. 'It's still dark, what time is it?'

'Six o'clock, sir. There has been another murder.'

Keemat looked hurt. 'What do you mean, Sant Ram? Mussoorie has never had more than one murder in a year!'

'I know, sir. I am very sorry.'

'Never mind. Who is it this time?'

'Chotte Lal.'

'You don't mean . . .'

'Yes, sir, the servant. He was found just after five o'clock, in the forest. He has been stabbed to death.'

Keemat groaned. 'I should have known something else would happen. There was too much calm—no one was worried, no one excited . . . All right, Sant Ram, go and fetch Dr Gulati while I get dressed. I'll meet you at the station house. Where did you say the body was found?'

'On the forest path, not far from the old lady's house—the Englishwoman Miss Bean.'

XV

Half an hour later, Inspector Keemat Lal, accompanied by Dr Gulati, Sant Ram and a photographer, was standing over the corpse of Chotte Lal, which lay sprawled across a narrow path. The sun had not yet risen, and there was an atmosphere of gloom and oppression in the dark forest.

Chotte had a knife in his back. The handle of the knife had a Tibetan design—common enough in Mussoorie. It stuck out from beneath the left shoulder blade. There were also knife wounds on his neck and arm. Chotte's shirt was drenched with blood and the heavy morning dew.

'He has been dead several hours,' said Dr Gulati, after making a cursory examination.

'He must have been killed late last night', said Keemat, as he stooped and went through Chotte's pockets. The pockets were empty, except for some loose change. But when Keemat turned the body over, he found a ring impressed in the soft earth. He held it up to the brightening horizon. It was a gold ring, with a beautiful pale blue amethyst in the centre, surrounded by four small diamonds.

'It looks like a valuable ring,' said the doctor.

'Yes. It's valuable. I think it belonged to the Rani.'

'Do you think this man had stolen it? But then why . . .' The doctor's voice trailed off into a puzzled undertone.

'I do not understand it myself,' said Keemat. 'If Chotte took the Rani's ring and killed her, why was *he* killed? Did he really take the ring? And if so, wouldn't he have hidden it or disposed of it somewhere? When we searched him after the Rani's murder, there was no ring on his person. But now it would seem that he had been keeping it in his shirt pocket all along—ridiculous! I can think of two possibilities. Either Chotte's murderer dropped it here by accident, or it was deliberately placed near Chotte so that the attack on him would appear to be the work of an accomplice.'

'It sounds very confusing.'

'Or, Chotte could have known who the Rani's murderer was. Possibly he was going to tell us something. Perhaps he was trying blackmail. Yes, that seems likely. The Rani's murderer wanted to silence Chotte, and placed the ring beside him in order to confuse the issue. I don't think the Rani was killed because of the ring—but perhaps someone would like us to think so . . . Well, this case is full of possibilities and probabilities. I wish we had not released Chotte in the beginning. We should have tortured him a little and made him talk—then we might have saved his life!'

'He was afraid to talk.'

'Yes . . . And there is someone else who is afraid to talk. Sant Ram, I want you to place a man on duty near the bania's shop. I want him to keep an eye on the girl. She knows something, and she may be in danger. We don't want a third murder! If little girls start getting killed, the name of the Mussoorie police will be mud. And now, my friends, I must leave you to the company of the corpse, while I pay another visit to Miss Bean, who so conveniently discovered the body at five o'clock this morning.'

XVI

The old lady was having her breakfast when Keemat presented himself at her front door. The discovery of a particularly bloody corpse appeared to have done little to diminish her appetite. She had finished a hard-boiled egg and two slices of toast with marmalade, and was almost through her second cup of coffee. She waved the Inspector to a chair.

'I hope you won't mind if I finish my breakfast,' she said. 'These early morning walks give me a ferocious appetite.'

Keemat sat down and waited patiently for Miss Bean to finish her coffee. Aware that breakfast had a sort of religious significance for the English, he maintained a discreet silence.

'Will you have some coffee?' she asked when she had finished.

Keemat said he had had two cups before leaving home, and politely declined the offer. It was as well that he did so, because Miss Bean, taking the lid off the coffeepot, observed, 'Anyway, there isn't any left,' and put the lid down again with an air of finality.

Keemat cleared his throat. 'I hope it wasn't a shock, madam, finding the body like that—and in such a mess!'

'Oh, bodies don't worry me,' said Miss Bean, her mouth full of toast. 'I was down south during the Moplah risings—that was before you were born, I expect—and I saw a lot of people badly cut up. Planters, tea-pickers, religious fanatics. My father turned the house into a first-aid post. But by the end of the week, it resembled a morgue . . . Still, I must admit it was a little disconcerting this morning to find a dead man in the middle of the path. For one thing, I couldn't get to the clump of lilies growing on the other side. I wanted them for my garden. Well, I suppose I can get them tomorrow. Anyway, this man was lying across the path just where it passes through a small ravine. I could tell he was dead without touching him. Mouth open. Eyes glazed. Dry blood. Stabbed in the back. Very unpleasant. So I walked up to the bania's shop and told them about it, and I suppose they got word to you.'

'Yes, madam, thanks to your prompt action. Did you recognize the man?'

'Oh yes, it was Chotte Lal, poor fellow. I've known him since he was a boy—long before he became the Rani's upaid servant—some even say her lover. He was a good boy, used to run errands for me at one time. Then, when he grew up and married, he started getting into all sorts of scrapes.'

'Did he become a thief?'

'No, he wasn't dishonest. I don't think he ever stole anything. But he had other weaknesses. He drank a lot, and gambled, and got into debt all over the place.'

'Don't you think he might have resorted to theft when his creditors became too pressing?'

'I suppose human beings can be capable of anything when their situation is desperate—including murder! But Chotte wasn't a thief by nature. The Rani came nearer to being one.'

Keemat did not have any more questions for Miss Bean. Even if she had seen someone during her morning walk, it would have been of little or no significance—by then Chotte had been dead several hours. His murder would appear to have shortened Keemat's list of suspects by one. Or was it possible that the two killings had no connection?

If a third murder occurred, Keemat might just as well hand in his resignation. There was no time for him to waste. He thanked the old lady for her help, bowed himself out of her small front room, and toiled up the slope to the bania's shop.

Kamla had been to the bazaar. Keemat met her in the road as she was returning home.

'Come here, Kamla,' he said. 'I want to talk to you.'

The girl came to him unwillingly. She seemed more afraid of him than of any potential murderer. Keemat wondered if his presence could really be so depressing.

'Listen, Kamla,' he said, 'you know that Chotte

Lal was killed last night?'

She looked up at him quickly, a little alarmed and slightly puzzled. Then she nodded, still remaining silent.

'Do you have any idea who killed him? Come, Kamla, you can speak to me freely. You need not be frightened of me or the police.'

She shook her head emphatically. Keemat found it difficult to resist the appeal of her large dark eyes. Her small mouth looked as though it would taste very sweet.

'All right,' he said. 'But you know that Chotte was the Rani's servant. And you know something about the Rani's death that you are not telling me. Well, I cannot force you to tell me what you know. But it is dangerous, little girl—it is dangerous to hide whatever it is that you are hiding. If the man who murdered the Rani is the same man who killed Chotte, then he will not hesitate to get rid of anyone else who knows something—who knows too much! Do you realize that? Do you realize the danger to yourself?'

She looked at him with unfeigned surprise. He did not see any fear in her eyes. But perhaps a doubt entered her mind, because she seemed on the verge of saying something. She opened her mouth as though to speak. Keemat felt his hands get clammy in nervous anticipation. Then she shut her mouth firmly, and shook her head again.

'So you have nothing to tell me?'

'There is nothing.' She said this with a certain reluctance, with a sort of sadness.

'Then let me warn you to be careful,' said Keemat kindly. 'But of course you must already realize that . . .' And then, to test the girl's reactions, he suddenly said, 'Was it the butcher?'

She took her time to answer, but that may have been because of the unexpectedness of the question. 'I do not know,' she said finally.

'Was it Mr Dalip Singh?'

She puckered up her brows. 'Who is Mr Dalip Singh?'

'Never mind. Was it Chotte?'

'I do not know.' There was no hesitation now.

'Was it Mrs Kapoor?'

She paused, considered the question, and said, very slowly, 'I do not know.'

Keemat waited a moment before asking, 'Was it the missionary?'

She shrugged her shoulders.

'Was it the old lady, Miss Bean?'

She smiled this time, grinned at Keemat with the tolerance one shows towards a second-rate circus clown who is doing his best. He cursed himself for putting this last question. The girl no longer took him seriously. She turned away. Her feet pattered down the path, and she disappeared round the bend.

Keemat glanced up the hillside. One of his constables, disguised as a grass cutter, was hacking away rather inexpertly at the sward. That, at least, was something. It meant the girl was safe for the time being.

XVII

Keemat felt very restless for the remainder of the morning. He hovered for some time in the vicinity of the Rani's house. He could see Mrs Kapoor hanging out her washing in her back garden. She looked up at him once, half-expecting him to come down and speak to her; but he had no more questions—or rather, none that could be answered by her.

The rhododendron trees were in flower, and there were tender green leaves on some of the fruit trees. The maple leaves were tongues of flame. Mrs Simmons waved to Keemat from her gate, and Keemat lifted his hand in response. A friendly sort of place, Mussoorie, when people weren't being axed to death.

A train of mules came trotting along the road,

and Keemat moved to the edge of the path to avoid them. But one of the mules brushed against his coat sleeve, and caught him off-balance. He stumbled into the stormwater drain, cursing the mule-driver. It was impossible to keep one's dignity on a narrow hill road!

He reached the Rani's house and stood at the gate, wondering if there was any point in going in. The place had been searched. But he knew that in any official search, no matter how conscientiously it was done, there were certain important elements which were not given enough importance—the atmosphere of the place, its smell and character, the way things were arranged, the way a person lived. Someone might die, but his or her personality lingered on where they had lived . . . And Keemat had never been alone in the Rani's house and had never been able to absorb its distinctive atmosphere. And he knew that it was important that he should do so. For the secret of the Rani's death lay in her life. She was the oppressor who had been turned into victim.

He wished he had known her personally. He wished he had been able to hate her as so many others had done. Then perhaps he would have known what it was like to want to kill her.

Or would he have hated her? Might he not have

liked her instead? Keemat often found himself taking a fancy to the most unlikely people. He pushed his way in through the creaking gate. The keys of the front door were in his pocket. He let himself into the empty house.

There was a musty smell in the rooms. Dust lay thick on the tables and chairs. The bed was bare, stripped of its coverings. Most of the Rani's personal things had been taken away by her brother the previous evening. There was nothing here that could help Keemat.

But how, he wondered, could a woman have lived alone in this dark echoing house, quarrelling with the rest of the world, eking out a living in dubious ways? She had been a queen once, albeit a rather shabby one, but nevertheless a queen. There had been people to do things for her and fulfil her demands. She must have been attractive once. It couldn't have been poverty that rankled with her as much as being ignored, and treated with the kind of indifference to which most other mortals were accustomed. She craved power even in her decline— power over people, over her friends and neighbours. Like Mussoorie itself, she was a faded queen in search of subjects . . .

Nothing to learn from the house. It was without character—it had long lost its charm and the removal of most of the Rani's possessions had depleted what remained of its distinctive nature.

Turning back to the front door, Keemat saw something glistening in a narrow crack near the frame of the door. He would not have noticed it if the morning sun had not been pouring in through the window, glinting off the little object. He stooped and picked up a piece of glass. It was part of a broken bangle.

Keemat took the fragment into the garden and turned it over in his hand. There was something familiar about its colour and design. Didn't Kamla wear similar glass bangles? And hadn't he noticed that she wore only two instead of the usual three on her wrist? Perhaps one of her bangles had broken and fallen here some time back, and had been swept into a corner where it had remained unnoticed for weeks. Kamla often came to the Rani's house with supplies from her father's shop. There was nothing unusual about her bangle being there. But how had the bangle broken?

On the garden path, near a flower bed, he found another piece from the same green bangle. Perhaps it had, after all, been broken quite recently. Well, his men had not been searching for bangles, nor did Keemat attach much significance to this find. Still, he was curious. He would speak to Kamla about it.

The girl was not at the bania's shop. Her father said she was a little way down the hill, gathering dry sticks for a fire while the cow grazed on the slopes.

Keemat decided to follow the narrow path down the hill. It went round a small outcrop of rock, dipped steeply through sorrel and cactus, and disappeared into a clump of maple trees. He found Kamla sitting at the edge of the forest, a bundle of twigs lying beside her.

She looked up at him with apprehension, and he smiled to try and reassure her. 'You are always wandering about alone,' he said. 'Don't you feel afraid?'

'It is safer when I am alone,' she replied. 'Nobody comes here.'

He glanced quickly at the bangles on her wrist, and noticed that they matched the broken piece. He held out the bit of coloured glass.

'I found it in the Rani's house,' he said. 'Your bangle must have broken when you were there.'

Kamla did not wait for him to finish what he was saying. With a look of pure terror in her eyes, she sprang up from the ground, swung around with a flounce of her skirts, and fled into the forest.

Keemat was completely taken aback. He had not expected such a reaction. Of what significance was the broken bangle? He hurried after Kamla, slipping on the smooth pine needles that carpeted the hillside. He was among the trees, looking about him, when he heard a stifled sob from behind a grassy knoll to his left. Turning, he saw the girl poised on the knoll, facing him. She had an axe in her hands.

When Kamala saw him looking up at her, she raised the axe above her shoulder with both hands. Then she rushed down the slope towards him.

Keemat was too astonished to be able to move aside. He stared open-mouthed as the girl rushed at him with the axe. The velocity of her attack would bring her right up against him, and the axe, in its descent, would crush his skull. But while she was still about six feet away, the axe flew out of her hands. It sprang into the air as though it had a life and impulse of its own, and flew at Keemat in a high swinging curve.

In spite of his bulk, Keemat moved swiftly aside. And the axe, grazing his shoulder, sank into the soft bark of the maple tree behind him.

Kamla sank down at his feet, weeping hysterically. And Keemat, instead of being furious and outraged, instead of seizing the girl and marching her off to the police station, placed his large hand gently on her head.

Perhaps it could only have happened in India—this sudden protective compassion for the person you are supposed to destroy.

'Tell me what happened,' said Keemat. 'Come, little girl, I will not harm you. Tell me everything.'

And she told him.

She told him how the Rani had called her to the house, and had given her tea and sweets. Dalip Singh had been there. After a while he had begun stroking her arms and knees with his fat hairy hands. She had drawn away, but Dalip Singh had pressed her against a corner of the wall. The Rani kept telling her not to be afraid, saying that Dalip Singh would take good care of her. Kamla had slipped under the man's outstretched arms and made a rush for the door. The Rani had caught her by the shoulders and pushed her back into the room. Kamla had seen the axe lying in a corner. She had pounced on it, raised it above her head, and advanced towards Dalip Singh. Realizing that he had gone too far, and valuing the symmetry of his neck, Dalip Singh had backed away from her and rushed out of the house. But the Rani, in a towering rage, had hurled abuse at the girl and sprung towards her; and Kamla, in panic and desperation, had brought the axe down across the Rani's forehead.

The Rani had fallen to the floor. And Kamla had fled from the house. Her bangle must have broken when she stumbled against the door.

Still carrying the axe, she had run into the forest. After concealing the axe beneath some ferns, she had lain weeping on the grass until it grew dark. But such was the strength of her nature and such the resilence of youth, that she had recovered sufficiently to be able to return home looking her normal self—and was able, during the following days, to maintain a stoic silence regarding the whole sordid affair . . .

Now, having found a shocked and sympathetic listener in Keemat Lal, Kamla poured out the tale. Her dark eyes still glistening with tears, she looked up at him appealingly.

'What will you do now?' she whispered.

Keemat was silent for a few moments, looking at her with a mixture of sadness and awe. 'I do not know,' he said sincerely. 'I do not know . . .'

XVIII

And for several days Keemat did absolutely nothing.

Something seemed to have happened to him in a deeply personal way. He was still aggressive with her subordinates; he drank as much as before; he ate heartily; but anyone who knew him well would have realized that he had come up against emotions he had not experienced before. What these new emotions were, he did not himself understand. Was it pity for Kamla that made him hold back in the matter? Or a knowledge that he would not be able to live with himself if he became the instrument of her incarceration in a remand home?

He would have closed the case even sooner had he not been worried about Dalip Singh. He was certain that Dalip Singh had killed the servant, Chotte.

It was not difficult to find a reason. Chotte, on his return from the bazaar where he had been doing the Rani's shopping, must have seen Dalip Singh rushing from the house. A few minutes later, Chotte had found the Rani dead, and must have quite naturally jumped to the conclusion that Dalip Singh was her murderer. He had not been willing to inform the police because he was afraid of Dalip Singh. Later, it may have occurred to him to blackmail the businessman. And Dalip Singh could not have called Chotte's bluff, because if he revealed the identity of the Rani's true killer, the story of his own reprehensible actions would come to light. His reputation and his family life would be ruined, and his business affairs would suffer. And so, on some pretext, he had probably accompanied Chotte along the path that led to the latter's living quarters very late at night. As they were crossing the ravine, he could have easily plunged the knife into Chotte's back.

In order to confuse the police, Dalip Singh must have dropped the Rani's ring near Chotte—a ring that the businessman had been holding as security against a loan made to her.

But Keemat had no evidence. He could only conjecture, based on the testimony of the girl. She could not testify without admitting her own guilt; and he had as yet no intention of exposing her.

XIX

Sometimes on the Mall, Keemat would meet Mrs Kapoor or the Simmonses or even Dalip Singh.

Mrs Kapoor always showed a most unwelcome interest in the progress of the case, and seemed to enjoy Keemat's obvious discomfiture. Perhaps she too had some inkling of the truth. 'It must have been an outsider,' she said consolingly. 'Otherwise, I am sure you would have found the murderer by now.'

The Simmonses did not mention the case, but greeted Keemat effusively and passed on their way. But he knew that they were thinking about it, and that in private they would be commenting on the inefficiency of the Mussoorie police force.

Dalip Singh, too, greeted him effusively; but the man was uneasy. Keemat could sense that Dalip Singh was puzzled by his inactivity and silence. What could it mean? Was the Inspector on to something, was he biding his time?

The weather was warming up, and people were beginning to come up to the hill station from the plains. The schools had opened. Sometimes Keemat, on his way to office, would pass Kamla on her way to school. At first, whenever she met him, she lowered her head and hurried on her way; and then, on one occasion, she looked up and met his eyes. What she saw in them must have given her confidence, because the next time she met Inspector Keemat Lal, she smiled.

Keemat was taken aback by her smile. He stopped, and patted her gently on the head. 'Are you all right?' he asked tenderly, almost as though he were talking to his own child.

'Yes,' she said, giving him a look of trust. 'I am all right.'

He stroked her dark smooth cheek, and allowed her to pass on.

And so sometimes when they met on the road, Keemat and the girl would stop to talk. And one evening, when he had finished his office work, and Kamla was on her way home, they sat down together on a bench beside the Mall, overlooking the Doon valley. Kamla pointed out several streams and told Keemat their names; and she described the forests that covered the surrounding hills, and the animals that roamed in them; and she told him the names of some trees, and when they shed their leaves and blossomed—she knew all these things which Keemat did not know. There were, he reflected, very few policemen who could tell a chestnut from a date palm, and he felt rather proud of his newly-acquired knowledge. But then, he should never have been a policeman.

People were beginning to forget about the murder of the Rani, although there were some who swore that her ghost walked the Mall on misty evenings. It was a pity about the servant; but the general opinion was that he had been involved in the murder, and that he had been done to death by an accomplice.

Keemat knew better, but he was not going to divulge his knowledge. The girl meant more to him than the lives of the Rani and Chotte Lal and Dalip Singh put together. The first two could not be brought back to life; and Dalip Singh, he felt sure, would meet with retribution one day. Keemat's outlook was fatalistic, and he had already resigned himself to the prospect of remaining an inspector for another three years.

The case was closed—or rather, the file was put in a pending tray.

Keemat's promotion was, as expected, postponed. But he got his transfer—to Shahpur, where, ironically, the enforcement of prohibition was to be one of his principal responsibilities.

His wife dutifully packed their belongings, while Keemat soaked up innumerable brandies in the bar of the Himalaya Hotel. Several times he spotted Kamla on the road, but as he was usually drunk at the time, he avoided her by taking a side road. It made him feel guilty to be drunk or smelling of liquor in her presence.

He wondered what Kamla had done with the axe. It had been left dangling in the tree the day she had tried to kill him. But it was too good an axe to be thrown away. Kamla must have taken it home. It was probably being used for chopping firewood.

XX

Keemat went to great pains to remain sober on the day of his departure. He was on the Mall when Kamla came down the road, her satchel of school books swinging from her thin shoulder.

'Namaste, uncle,' she said when she saw him. Recently she had taken to calling Keemat 'uncle'.

'Hullo, Kamla. Are you all right?'

'I am all right, uncle.'

Keemat nodded benevolently, but he was looking a little depressed. 'I am going away tomorrow,' he said. 'I have to leave Mussoorie. But you will be all right, don't worry. There is nothing to be afraid of. Just keep away from Dalip Singh.'

She said nothing, but looked out over the hills, at a distant plume of smoke.

'Is it a forest fire?' asked Keemat.

'No, it's a train,' she said. 'Will you be going in the train?'

'Yes,' he said.

'I have never travelled in a train,' said Kamla.

Keemat did not know what to say. Suddenly, and for no tangible reason, he could not bear the thought of leaving Mussoorie. He shared a secret with Kamla, and he felt that in this way he was sharing something of her life. This feeling of intimacy was something new to him—exhilarating and fresh— it made him feel youthful. And perhaps, after all, he was not so old . . .

'I should never have been a policeman,' he said. He stroked the girl's cheek, and hurried away.

XXI

When Keemat Lal finished telling me this story, there was a distant, rather sentimental look in his eyes.

'It didn't turn out very well for you,' I remarked sympathetically.

'No,' he said. 'Here I am in Shahpur without any prospects. But tell me, Mr Bond, what would you have done had you been in my place?'

I pondered his question for a moment or two, then said, 'I suppose it would have depended on how much I cared about the girl.'

'Then you would have put your personal feelings above your duty to uphold the law?'

'Yes, I think so. I believe justice is greater than the law. And I believe personal loyalties come first—if they don't, we are doomed as human beings.'

He seemed relieved at this sincere expression of my own philosophy and outlook.

'Still,' I said, 'it's a pity that Dalip Singh got off so easily.'

'Oh, he didn't get off altogether. He got into trouble later on for swindling some manufacturing concern, and went to jail for a couple of years. Section 420. His business affairs suffered, and his wife, fed up with his ways, returned to her parents. He is out now, but he is not the same man. He is ruined financially.'

The beer bottles were all empty, and Keemat Lal got up to leave.

His last words to me were, 'I should never have been a policeman.'

A few days later I found a buyer for my property, and let it go cheap. After leaving Shahpur, I did not hear of Inspector Keemat Lal again, but I hope he got a promotion and a decent transfer. A man of his compassion deserved something better than Shahpur.